W9-AJP-463

Advance Praise for *You Bet Your Life*

"The irony of Spencer's heart-wrenching yet courageous story is that he had so little to gain, so much to lose. His is a well-written documentary of a life that started from meager beginnings, grew to one of recognition among the elites, and came tumbling down because of the unconscious, insatiable quest for something that was already there, because it must come from within."

—L. Douglas Wilder, former governor of Virginia

"In Spencer Christian's story, you get to know a man as he learns to know himself. And he is someone worth getting to know."

—Gil Gross, network radio news commentator
and former news correspondent for the ABC Radio Networks

"The soothing voice of Spencer Christian, familiar and cheerfully bidding 'Good morning, America' from our television sets at daybreak, now clearly speaks to us from the pages of his compelling book. With heart and humor he parts the curtain of his life as a beloved TV personality, providing a rare and raw look behind the scenes to witness the addiction that ripped at his family and career."

—Squire Rushnell, former Vice President, Daytime Television, ABC

"If you want to know what a moral wakeup call feels like, read this book. Spencer gives us a very transparent self-disclosure about the racial, celebrity, and addiction issues he experienced, and how family, faith, values, and character enabled survival in the darkest times. I know this man to be a man of his word. When he says that he has been there and done that and is now ready to ring some purpose bells, I believe him and support him and hope that many will find courage from his testimony."

—Irving R. Stubbs, author and retired Presbyterian minister

Also by Spencer Christian

Spencer Christian's Geography Book

Spencer Christian's Weather Book

*Electing Our Government: Everything You Need
to Know to Make Your Vote Really Count*

*Can It Really Rain Frogs?
The World's Strangest Weather Events*

*Is There a Dinosaur in Your Backyard?
The World's Most Fascinating Fossils,
Rocks, and Minerals*

*Shake, Rattle, and Roll:
The World's Most Amazing Volcanoes,
Earthquakes, and Other Forces*

*What Makes the Grand Canyon Grand?
The World's Most Awe-Inspiring Natural Wonders*

$ 26. 00

3 1489 00713 0535

YOU
BET
YOUR
LIFE

How I Survived Jim Crow Racism, Hurricane Chasing, and Gambling

SPENCER
CHRISTIAN

A POST HILL PRESS BOOK

You Bet Your Life:
How I Survived Jim Crow Racism, Hurricane Chasing, and Gambling
© 2018 by Spencer Christian
All Rights Reserved

ISBN: 978-1-68261-639-0
ISBN (eBook): 978-1-68261-640-6

Cover art by Dan Pitts
Cover photo by Tanya Constantine
Interior Design and Composition, Greg Johnson, Textbook Perfect

No part of this book may be reproduced, stored in a retrieval system,
or transmitted by any means without the written permission of the
author and publisher.

Post Hill Press
New York • Nashville
posthillpress.com

Published in the United States of America

Acknowledgments

So many people and institutions have played significant roles in shaping my life and career that I could fill the pages of an entire book with their names. In the interest of time and space, I will acknowledge some, without whom this book would not have been possible.

Spencer, Sr., and Lucy Christian for being the world's greatest parents and the very definition of love.

Lutrell Christian, my "little brother" and childhood playmate.

Jason Christian and Jessica Christian, my amazing children and the greatest sources of joy in my life—before my grandchildren. ☺

Rev. George W. Watkins, Elam Baptist Church, and the amazing teachers at Ruthville School for guidance and direction during my formative years in Charles City County, Virginia.

Hampton University for a rich educational experience.

Doug Hill, news director and mentor at WWBT-TV, who gave me my first job.

Ron Kershaw, news director at WBAL-TV, a brilliant and visionary television executive.

ABC Television, Inc., and ABC News for more than 40 years of continuous employment, and for being supportive during my personal challenges.

Good Morning America executives SQuire Rushnell, George Merlis, Phil Beuth, and Jack Reilly for providing me with such a rich and fulfilling career experience.

KGO-TV for being my current and supportive home in the ABC family.

Ralph Mann, Steve Pinkus, and Cynthia Riley for their friendship and dedicated service as my agents at various times in my career.

Jay Shaw, my longtime friend and business manager.

All of the producers, field producers, writers, editors, camerapersons, technicians, directors, stage managers, maintenance staff, makeup artists, and security guards who have assisted me, encouraged me, and "made me look good."

Charlie Gibson and Joan Lunden for friendship, partnership, and an incredible personal and professional journey.

Antonia Felix, my editor and friend, without whose guidance, encouragement, inspiration, and brilliant insight I could not have written this book.

Chapter One

Who needs drugs when you've got a pair of hot dice in your hands? Not me! On that cool October night in Atlantic City, I was on fire. I had just scorched the craps tables at Caesars and the Showboat for about $10,000 each, and now I was in the middle of a monster roll at the most exclusive joint in town, Trump Plaza. The casino was a dazzling tower of gold, brass, and crystal chandeliers, but at this moment all eyes were on me. I was the "shooter," and all the players at this high-stakes table were cheering me on. Everyone in the room felt that they knew me, not just because I was in their homes every morning as the *Good Morning America* weatherman, but also because I was a familiar face at the casinos. The crowd of onlookers had grown so raucous that the security guards were keeping them a good distance from the table. When my "roll" finally ended, I received a huge round of applause from the crowd. I tipped the dealers $500 and gave $100 to each of the security guards who escorted me to the cashier's window, where I cashed in another $20,000.

Words cannot describe the excitement I felt at that moment. My hands were planted firmly in my pockets as I walked briskly out of the casino, protecting the $40,000 I had won in just two hours at the craps tables. My heart was pounding as I approached the private elevator, which would take me up to my comped luxury suite, where my wife, Diane, and kids, Jessica and Jason, were asleep. Could life be any better? Before my big score in the casinos, I had treated my family to a fabulous dinner at Trump Plaza's top gourmet restaurant. The following night, my 12-year-old son, Jason, and I would have ringside VIP seats for Mike Tyson's heavyweight title defense against Tyrell Biggs. And in just a few hours—as it was now around 2:00 a.m.—I would do my *Good Morning America* broadcast *live* in the very ring where the big fight would take place. My interview guests, in order of appearance, would be Donald Trump, whose hotel was hosting the fight; Don King, the flamboyant boxing promoter; Robin Givens, at that time Tyson's fiancée; and Kevin Rooney, Tyson's trainer.

I was absolutely on top of the world—invincible—or so I thought.

The life I had at that moment was so far removed from the adversity I had faced as a poor, black kid in the rural, segregated South that those early years seemed almost like a distant dream—like something from another lifetime. I was now on national TV for two hours every weekday morning, soon to be earning a seven-figure salary, and blessed with a lifestyle that exemplified the American Dream. And, oh yes, I was a high roller. This meant that casino-hotels from Las Vegas to Atlantic City to the Caribbean Islands offered me the finest luxury suites, gourmet meals with thousand-dollar bottles of wine, first-class air travel, and on-the-spot limousine service—all in exchange for a few hours a day of "action" at their gaming tables, which I was more than willing to provide. I had convinced myself that

I was simply enjoying an expensive form of recreation. But I was soon to realize that I was flirting with a dangerous and destructive narcotic—one that would eventually wreck my family, my finances, and my future on national television. My experience in Atlantic City on that October weekend in 1987 was an early warning.

One of the fringe benefits of my job was that I got to do "remotes" at major sports and entertainment events around the country, and I was often able to take my family along. The Tyson-Biggs fight was one of those occasions. On the morning of my *GMA* broadcast, my wife and kids were on location with me as I conducted my interviews in the boxing ring. They were thrilled to be there watching me schmooze with "The Donald," joke with Don King about his outrageous hair, and pose sensitive questions to Ms. Givens about her unlikely relationship with Tyson. I felt truly thankful for the privilege of providing my family with this special experience, and I loved seeing how excited Jason was as he looked forward to sitting with me ringside that night, just four rows away from the most feared and formidable fighter on the planet. But as the day dragged on and I looked for ways to kill time with Diane and the kids before that night's main event, I was thinking beyond the fight. I wanted to get back "in action." As Jason and I were ushered to our seats in the Atlantic City Convention Center—past the camera crews, the countless celebrities, and the aging high rollers whose hairpieces were older than the women they had hired to be their dates—I was rooting for a first-round knockout so I could return to the casino!

Mike Tyson didn't quite deliver the early ending I was hoping for. Tyrell Biggs somehow managed to elude Tyson's explosive knockout punch for six rounds, and I was growing restless. "Will you please knock this guy out," I was thinking as the seventh round began. I wanted, I *needed*, to get back to the craps tables—the scene of my own knockout performance the night before. Finally, just over two minutes into the seventh round, Tyson delivered the big left hook that would send Biggs to the canvas and me to the casino. Jason and I began plowing our way through the crowd while exclaiming our amazement at how long Biggs had survived Tyson's onslaught. It took us about 20 minutes to get out of the building, but it seemed like hours to me. I was itching for action. I escorted Jason up to the suite, kissed my family goodnight, and rushed down to the casino at Trump Plaza to pick up where I had left off the night before. But it didn't quite work out as I had planned.

Before I made my first bet of the night, it occurred to me that I should pay off the outstanding balances on a couple of my casino credit lines. I would have done that the night before, but I wanted to savor the feeling of those wads of cash in my pockets. Now I had to part with $25,000 of my newfound fortune, as the credit markers I'd signed on my previous trip to Atlantic City were approaching their deposit date, when they would be presented to my bank for payment from my checking account, and I certainly didn't want the people at my bank to know that I owed that kind of money to casinos. So, I paid off $15,000 at The Claridge Hotel and $10,000 at Caesars. And then, just before I headed back to Trump Plaza for some action, I had one of my few rational thoughts of the entire weekend: "Why not be happy with the $15,000 in winnings I still have in my pocket, go up to the suite, get a good night's sleep, and head home tomorrow knowing I have won this bout with the casinos?" No! I wouldn't be happy with the feeling that my winnings had shrunk, so I was determined to build my now-diminished bankroll back up to at least $20,000.

As I rode the escalator at Trump Plaza from the hotel's ground-floor entrance up to the casino, I had an uneasy feeling. It was eerie—like I was entering enemy territory. I looked around for a craps table that seemed to be "hot," where the players appeared to be winning, but none was to be found. At every table, I saw only somber faces. Craps can be that kind of game. When your numbers aren't showing up on the dice, your money just melts away and the game sucks all the fun out of you. But a hot shooter can turn defeat into delight in a matter minutes, and I wanted to be that shooter. I approached a half-empty table and claimed my spot. Rather than put my pocket cash into play, I signed a marker for $7,500 so I could play off "the casino's money."

That table remained as cold as ice! It took me only about three minutes to set up $900 in bets across the table, and then the dreaded seven appeared on the dice and wiped out all of my bets. My roll had ended. Shooter after shooter rolled the dice with the same outcome—I set up bets on three or four numbers, hoping for one or two of them to repeat, and *boom*, that damned seven would show up again and my chips were gone. When the $7,500 from that first marker dwindled to just over $1,000, it was time for me to try another table.

I had the depressing feeling that it might not be my night, but thought surely *some* of the previous night's sizzle must still have been in me. The dice couldn't remain cold forever! I was doing my best to muster up some confidence as I chose another table, where I immediately signed a second $7,500 marker. I had now withdrawn the amount of my entire credit line, $15,000, at Trump Plaza. I made only modest bets as the three shooters ahead of me rolled the dice. They didn't seem to project that winning look, so I wanted to reserve the big bets for my turn.

I had made a wise decision. Those guys ahead of me sucked. (This is how craps players think about shooters who cost them money.) Now, the dice were finally in my hand. Displaying confidence, I placed a starting bet that was three times larger than what I had bet on the previous shooters. One of them had apparently witnessed my big score the night before, and he loudly encouraged the other players to "load up" on me because, "This guy really knows how to roll them bones!" He was obviously convincing, as they all increased their bets—and I began to reward them. I was rolling repeating numbers without the seven showing up, and the table was beginning to make some money. All of a sudden, positive energy was building and players were yelling out the numbers they wanted me to roll. Each time I delivered a winner, loud cheers and clumsy high-fives erupted around the table. But I wasn't celebrating yet. Despite the growing chip stacks in front of the other players, my stack remained virtually unchanged, because I was using a bet progression system, which meant I was increasing my bets with each winning roll of the dice. And I was now at that critical point where I needed just one of my big bets to pay off, and I could rake in a couple of thousand dollars.

I shook the dice gently in my right hand and gave them a vigorous roll along the green felt tabletop. "Aw, *crap!*" (not to be confused with "craps") I exclaimed. The dice had delivered disappointment. They showed a five and a two—I had "sevened" out. And while the other players were happy to have won a few hundred dollars on their flat bets, I had actually lost a few hundred, because my roll had not lasted quite long enough for my bet progression to pay off. I gave the celebrants a forced smile and walked away.

"Dejection" is too mild a word to describe my feeling. My stomach felt nervous and queasy. Could my luck remain lousy all night? I had lost more than half of the $15,000 I had taken out in markers, so I decided to cash in the remaining chips—rather than make a partial payment on my credit line—just to have the feeling of more money in my pocket as I considered a change of venue. I walked out of Trump Plaza into the crisp autumn breeze, feeling a bit refreshed. My gambler's instincts told me to hop a cab over to the Showboat casino, where I had won $10,000 the night before. It was far enough from Trump Plaza that perhaps I could settle down and regain my composure during the ride.

*   *   *

It was a lively scene at the Showboat that night. Unlike the somber mood at the preceding joint, the craps tables were abuzz with talk about the fight—which, to me, now seemed like a distant memory.

"Can you believe Biggs lasted seven rounds with that monster?"

"Aw, man, Tyson was just playing with that boy. He didn't want to take him out too early."

I needed this kind of banter to remind me why I had made this trip to AC in the first place. It also made me remember how powerful I had felt after beating up the casinos just 24 hours earlier. I was now ready to swing into action again.

I called for a $15,000 marker—my full credit limit at the Showboat. I wanted to start with lots of chips in front of me for that feeling of power. But despite my momentary surge of confidence, the dice refused to roll my way. The curse of Trump Plaza had followed me all the way across town. For nearly an hour, the same old pattern prevailed—I'd build up my bets and seven out; build them up again, seven out again. It defied the laws of averages. Yes, the house had a fixed mathematical edge, but it wasn't supposed to bite me in the butt on every bet I made! I cashed in my few remaining chips and bolted. I was mad at myself and at the entire gambling universe.

It was now after 2:00 a.m.; the big fight was yesterday's news. And while my wife and kids were no doubt sleeping peacefully in the suite, I was walking rapidly and nervously through the streets of Atlantic City, past hookers and derelicts—the homeless and the hopeless—wondering if I had any more dignity than they did at that moment. I wasn't sure.

✳ ✳ ✳

Without any clear plan of action, I ended up at Caesars—not quite the equal of its older, more celebrated sibling in Las Vegas, but one of the classier casinos on the Atlantic City ("AC") boardwalk. Before storming the craps tables there, I took a moment to assess the night's self-inflicted damage. I still had $15,000 in my pockets from the previous night's winnings, plus a few thousand more after cashing in chips from unpaid markers. But my total loss for this night was over $20,000—more than half the amount I had won the night before. And having now blown through two of my previously paid-off credit lines, I no longer felt like a winner for this trip.

I stopped at a lively Caesars craps table and took out a $10,000 marker. The shooter was in the middle of his roll, and it was apparent that he had been rolling winning numbers. I jumped right in, placing sizable bets on five, six, eight, and nine, the numbers with the highest mathematical probability of showing up—other than seven, that is. I thought my bad luck might be ending as I collected about $1,500 in winnings before that guy sevened out. It was a relatively small amount in relation to my total loss for the night, but it was a confidence builder. Surprisingly, the next shooter declined his turn. He passed the dice to me, because he had seen me in action the night before and he wanted to ride a winning horse. That also boosted my confidence!

But what do craps players know? I ended up having the worst possible roll. I tossed the dice just enough times for players—including me—to get their chips set up on the pass line, come bets, and proposition bets, and then I rolled the hated seven. All of our bets were swept away, and a chorus of groans arose from the table. It was painful, and the pain got worse. In what seemed like no time at all, $5,000 worth of my chips had found its way into the stacks that belonged to the casino. I picked up my remaining $5,000 and headed for the blackjack tables. Of course, blackjack! I needed a change of games!

The first game I ever played in a casino was blackjack. It was back in the spring of 1978, after I had read a couple of books on card counting, a mathematically proven system designed to equip the studious to beat the game of casino blackjack. There were documented cases of card counters who were so successful that casinos had barred them from playing. Some of them had written instructional books, and I was their newest disciple. I studied the systems at home, late into the night, dealing out sample hands and practicing the techniques. And I had a successful two-year run in Vegas and AC, until I began to catch heat from casino executives who were onto me. So, I then gravitated to the more exciting, and more seductive, game of craps.

But in dark moments like this one at Caesars, blackjack offered me the best chance to reverse my fortunes. Plus, now that I was a high roller, my betting pattern was nothing like that of a typical card counter, so the pit bosses would welcome my action. I walked with supreme confidence to an empty table in the high-limit blackjack pit and carefully arranged my chip stacks according to denominations of $25, $100, and $500. The pit boss seemed uninterested, so I began betting and the dealer began dealing.

What came next was the worst sequence of hands I had ever seen. When I had 20, the dealer had 21. When I was dealt blackjack, it was just a push, as the dealer also had blackjack. When I took a hit with 12, I would get a 10 and go bust. And when I signaled "stay" with 18 or 19, the dealer would hit his 16 and draw a 5. My remaining $5,000 disappeared faster at blackjack than the first $5,000 had vanished at craps.

At this point, I gave in to desperation. Having used up the chips from my credit line, I dug into my pocket and pulled out $10,000 in cash—cash that I had vowed would not leave my pocket. And now that the money was out of my pocket, it was in play, but I wouldn't let it play here at Caesars. Instead, I held it tightly in my fist and dashed two blocks over to Trump Plaza, where the night's action had begun. Gamblers never lose hope, as long as they have a bankroll.

*   *   *

It was now 4:00 a.m., and I was hoping to make a quick score before heading up to the suite. If I could win back just a few thousand, I could get rid of that sick loser feeling that had overcome me, and I'd be able to go upstairs and sleep peacefully for a few hours with my family before heading home after breakfast.

As I approached the craps table, I could see that the dealers had changed shifts. None of the faces were the same as those I had seen there a few hours earlier. This felt like a good thing—new faces, new feeling, new luck!

Wrong. That $10,000 had the shelf life of a crumb in an ant-infested pantry. As the night became morning, the other players drifted away and I played out my few remaining chips alone—until I was numbed by the pain of losing. I then turned away from the table and, staring blankly ahead, walked to the VIP elevator. It was reserved for high rollers, but at that moment I felt like the lowest form of life. I tiptoed into my suite just before 5:00 a.m., kissed Diane and the kids gently on their foreheads, and climbed quietly into bed. I said my prayers, which I had done every night of my life, and asked God to comfort me. I didn't know what else to ask for. It was difficult to close my eyes. It was impossible to sleep. In just over 24 hours, I had turned $40,000 in winnings into a net loss. I felt worthless.

I tossed and turned until about 8:00 a.m., when everyone began waking up at once. I tried to put on a happy face for Jason and Jessica as I placed our room service order, but Diane instinctively knew that I'd had a losing night—a really bad one. I had no appetite for breakfast, but I forced down a waffle and some fruit, hoping it would make me feel better. It didn't. Soon, we were on our way down to the VIP lounge to check out and board our limo for the two-hour-and-fifteen-minute ride home. It was the longest, most depressing ride I can remember. Diane and the kids napped most of the way home, which gave me time to think about what the hell was wrong with me.

This was not the first time I had gambled all night and lost as much as some people earn in a year. And, in this case, I had started with such a huge amount in winnings that I could have stopped at almost any point and still have walked away a winner. This was not fun. It was not harmless recreation. I had never felt greater shame and self-loathing than I did at that moment. But I also knew that I did not want to stop gambling. In fact, I was already thinking ahead to how I'd come up with the cash to pay down my casino credit lines on the next trip, and how I'd definitely quit while ahead next time.

We finally arrived home, with much of the weekend still left to enjoy with my family. This would help get my mind off the events of Friday night. As the kids watched TV in the family room that afternoon and Diane and I discussed dinner plans, she asked me if I wanted to talk about Atlantic City. I was too embarrassed to give her the details, but told her I had gone from being a big winner to being a modest loser. I didn't have to say anything more. She could see my pain. She then said something to me in the kindest, most loving tone—words that have haunted me to this very day. She said, "God doesn't want you to be a gambler."

Chapter Two

Gambling had not always been a part of my life. In fact, I was nearly thirty years old, about six years into my TV career, when I was first bitten by the gambling bug. I had not yet arrived on the national stage at *GMA*, but was working at the ABC flagship station in New York. Some of my newsroom colleagues started a Friday-night poker game following the 11 p.m. news. It seemed like harmless fun to me. After all, my wife and young son would usually be asleep by the time I got home from work, so why not play cards for a couple of hours with my buddies? This is where my downward spiral began.

Within a matter of months, the friendly poker game had grown into a high-stakes battle in which hundreds—sometimes thousands—of dollars exchanged hands at each session. Occasionally, a single night's losses would be greater than a player's ability to pay right there on the spot, so we began keeping written records and exchanging IOUs. Within a year, I had lost several thousand dollars. And what had started as a relaxing way to unwind at the end of the workweek had become a cutthroat contest that lingered into Saturday mornings. The more desperate the losing players were to recoup their losses, the longer the game dragged on. I would sometimes get home so late the next morning that Diane and Jason were already awake.

I felt guilty and ashamed. Nothing meant more to me than my family. That is truly how I felt in my heart. My greatest joy was spending time with Diane and Jason, and now our precious family was about to grow larger. The birth of little Jessica was just a few months away. Diane was very thoughtful in her occasional suggestions that I might be letting poker drag me down and that my family would soon need me more than ever. So why was I allowing myself to fall into this abyss? In the face of nearly every important challenge in my life, I had been able to think rationally and do the right thing. Why not now? I seriously needed to clean up my act.

During the next few months, before my daughter's birth in the spring of 1978, I began to pull away from poker. Going home after work and getting a full night's sleep enabled me to be a more energetic and connected husband and father. I also had more money to spend on family fun, because I wasn't pissing away my paycheck at poker. Little did I know that poker had merely been my gateway drug.

On Memorial Day weekend in 1978, casino gambling came to Atlantic City, New Jersey, with the opening of America's first legal casino outside Nevada. I couldn't wait to check it out. At this point, I had not yet visited the "gambling capital"—Las Vegas—but why bother with a five-hour flight when Atlantic City was just a two-hour drive? So, leaving Diane and the kids at home, I drove down to AC to meet an old friend for a guys' weekend of gambling.

There was no poker, but I found a tantalizing array of other games: blackjack, craps, roulette, slots, and more. The atmosphere was electric, and I was ready to be plugged in. But despite my revved-up excitement and eagerness to play, the effect of this first casino experience seemed rather benign. That weekend of fun ended up costing me only a couple of hundred dollars, which didn't seem like a big deal, and I returned home feeling unharmed. I did, however, have a growing appetite for more action.

* * *

Shortly after my little Atlantic City adventure, Diane and I took our first trip to Las Vegas. It was a true vacation: we went to shows, ate gourmet meals, did some shopping, and, of course, I gambled. I behaved like a normal person—I didn't spend every waking hour in the casino, and I had luck on my side. During the three-day trip, I won a total of $1,400—which more than covered our vacation expenses, and I came home with a wad of winnings.

Over the next few years, the casinos became my playground—usually with my family in tow. You see, this is how I legitimized my growing habit. Taking my wife and kids to fancy meals and glamorous shows "entitled" me to some late-night fun at the blackjack tables. At this point, I had also learned to play another "game." By opening casino credit lines and playing at higher stakes, I was able to qualify for what is known in the gambling world as RFB comps—room, food, and beverages were complimentary, along with VIP seats in the showrooms and ringside tickets at championship boxing matches. In my mind, I didn't have a gambling problem; I was simply enjoying an expensive form of recreation.

By 1984, six years after my first casino experience, I was in deep trouble. I had maxed out my casino credit lines, was drowning in bank loans and credit card debt, and was behind in federal income taxes. While my career was on the upswing and my family life was richly rewarding, I was in a quiet state of panic. The IRS had refused a settlement offer and placed a lien against my personal property. A short time later, when my paycheck didn't arrive on payday, I discovered that the IRS had attached (garnished) my wages. And just when I thought things could not get worse, a man in a dark suit tacked a notice on the front door of my house, stating that the Internal Revenue Service had seized my property. This happened in broad daylight, in full view of my neighbors, and was now a matter of public record.

I had never felt more helpless and humiliated. My kids overheard their friends talking about me at school. "His dad is Spencer Christian, that guy on the news. The IRS is taking their house. They have to move." A notice of the forced sale of our property appeared in the Sunday newspaper. Whenever I went out with my family, I imagined that people were talking about us. I could almost feel the stares and hear the whispers. I did my best to put on a happy face, at work and at home, but I felt like a broken man inside—not just because of my financial misery, but because I had done this to myself. I was not a victim of anyone else's schemes. I had chosen this poisonous path, and the most painful part was that I was dragging my wife and kids along with me.

After a series of exhausting meetings with the IRS examiner, my attorney advised me that my only recourse was bankruptcy. So, in November 1984, I filed for Chapter 7. Now, I was ravaged with fear. I could not sleep at night. I was a public figure—a prominent TV newscaster. Could negative publicity surrounding the bankruptcy cause me to lose my job? What would my kids think of me? How would my wife deal with this? And, of course, how could I show my face in public? After all, pride was a factor too.

Much to my surprise and delight, Diane was a tower of strength and loving support during this ordeal. And fortunately, Jason and Jessica were too young to recognize the full gravity of the situation, so Mom and Dad were able to reassure them that everything would be okay. The IRS released the wage attachment after seizing our house, so I began receiving paychecks again and was able to move my family into a rental property. And my job insecurity was erased when the bankruptcy proceedings concluded with no negative repercussions at work. I thanked God for this second chance. I wasn't suddenly on Easy Street—my debt burden was not completely erased, and I still had to pay off settlements with several creditors. But I had my family, my health, and my job. Now, my personal challenge was to quit gambling.

During this time of rejoicing and relief, I could not have imagined that darker days were yet to come. But the mind of an addict can play cruel tricks—the cruelest, perhaps, on the addict himself.

Chapter Three

My parents would have died of heartbreak had they discovered how far I'd strayed from their guidance and direction. I had truly become the prodigal son.

Spencer, Sr., and Lucy Christian were poor, rural, hard-working, God-fearing people who had grown up during the Great Depression. They faced all the harsh indignities that were part of everyday life for black people in the Old South. My dad and his brothers were in that generation of young African American men who put their lives on the line in World War II—serving in a racially segregated US military—and returned home to a country that still treated them like second-class citizens, denying them the basic freedoms they had fought to preserve for the rest of America. Yet, despite the unspeakable hardships they endured, my parents were firm believers in the American Dream. Guided by their unshakable faith in the God who had delivered our forefathers from slavery, they invested their prayers and hard work in the hope that their children would experience a better America.

It's remarkable that my parents were able to instill their positive, hopeful worldview in my brother and me. I was born in

1947, just two years after the war ended. By the time I was four years old, I had become aware that there were places I couldn't go and things I couldn't touch, because I was black. When we went shopping at department stores like Sears or Woolworth, my parents cautioned me that we couldn't use the clean, shiny water fountain under the sign saying WHITES ONLY. We had to use the one that was older and smaller, labeled COLORED. The same rule applied to restrooms. Being rather perceptive and inquisitive, I recall asking my parents why the stores always let the "colored" facilities get so rusty and run-down, while keeping the "white" ones clean and modern-looking. I can still see their pained expressions as they tried to explain that black people didn't have equal rights yet, but it wouldn't take long, because our country was "moving in the right direction."

Jim Crow segregation meant much more than separate restrooms and water fountains. Most of the stores in which we shopped provided no food service for blacks at all. Lunch counters were strictly for whites. So, after spending their hard-earned money on household needs, school supplies, or clothing, my parents couldn't buy a hamburger and a soda in those stores—not even at the takeout counter. Buying clothes and shoes could be humiliating as well. Usually, black customers were not permitted to try on a clothing item. Nothing was allowed to go on our bodies and remain in the store. We simply bought what we thought was the right size and hoped it would fit properly when we got home.

There were some exceptions to this practice. I noticed at an early age that Jewish merchants generally seemed kinder and friendlier to blacks. In fact, there was a shoe store in downtown Richmond, Virginia, with a very common Jewish name, and the salesmen there would always bring out several pairs of shoes for us to try on, just to make sure we had the right fit before we paid for anything. This left a strong and positive impression on me, as I began to recognize at an early age that most Jewish establishments did not practice racial discrimination. When I was a child, black kids were not allowed to use public playgrounds, tennis courts, or swimming pools, but we could go to the Jewish Community Center. The JCC did not discriminate, but the rest of my childhood world did, and every day the signs of separation reminded me to "stay in my place." By the time I was about twelve, however, I began to connect my experiences with Jewish people to something larger. I observed that many Jews were at the forefront of the civil rights movement—being beaten and arrested, some even killed, along with blacks—and that one of the hallmarks of Jewish culture was standing up for human dignity and social justice.

On a typical Saturday, when my family went shopping, we would make the half-hour drive from our home in rural Charles City County to Richmond, which was the nearest city. My parents would always remind my little brother, Lutrell, and me to "empty" ourselves before we left home, because there would be no service stations or restaurants along our rural drive that would let us use their restrooms. If nature called, my dad would have to pull over so we could run into the woods and relieve ourselves. By the way, emptying ourselves at home meant going to the stinky, old outhouse. Remember, we were poor, rural Southerners. We didn't have an indoor toilet until I was twelve years old, so relieving ourselves at home was not always a comfortable experience.

On the way home from the city after our Saturday shopping, if we were hungry or just wanted a snack, my dad would stop at one of the few fast-food places that had a separate outdoor window for "coloreds" to get sandwiches and sodas to go. I felt sad watching my parents suffer this humiliation, but they always put such a positive spin on these situations that my brother and I felt reassured. They constantly reminded us that the civil rights movement was growing stronger and stronger, the racial barriers would be coming down, and we would soon have equal rights.

One of the many remarkable things about my mom and dad is how they always made home a safe and special place. And "home" didn't just mean the house in which we lived. Whenever and wherever we were together, that was home. Even though I was aware in my childhood years that innocent black people were physically attacked—even killed—for no reason other than pure racial hatred, I never felt unsafe or frightened when we were at home. I remember how I prayed every day for my parents' safety and well-being, because they made me feel loved, protected, and valued.

* * *

My worldview regarding race and racism changed dramatically in the summer of 1960 when I turned thirteen years old. Prior to that summer, the longest distance we had traveled from our home in central Virginia was to Washington, D.C., about 95 miles from our house. But that year we were going up North on a family vacation. We packed up the car and drove to East Orange, New Jersey, where we spent a week with Uncle Carey (my dad's brother) and Aunt Dot. We had never been up North before, but we knew that once we left the South, we would find public facilities that were integrated. It was hard to imagine what that would be like. Before this trip, we had seen racially integrated restaurants, movie theaters, and playgrounds only on TV. I was both nervous and excited.

As we made the drive northward through Washington, Maryland, Delaware, and into New Jersey, I felt like a free person—a regular American—for the first time in my life. It was absolutely exhilarating! There were no WHITES ONLY signs, and when we stopped for food we were served and treated just like everyone else. During our stay with Uncle Carey, we went to the movies, restaurants, and a public amusement park. These were simple pleasures we could not enjoy back home in Virginia. One evening after dinner at Uncle Carey's, a neighbor took us bowling. It was our first time in a bowling alley, and I guess we expected people to stare at us or give us angry looks, something we encountered nearly every day in the South. But when that didn't happen, we felt right at home. My brother, parents, and I thought we were in a fantasyland. I had never been happier.

But the drive home at the end of the week was a different story. The closer we got to Virginia, the lower our spirits dropped. Lutrell and I tried to make a game out of it, which we called "Countdown to Segregation." As we left southern New Jersey and crossed into Delaware, we said, "Two more states to segregation." After crossing from Delaware into Maryland, "One more state to segregation." By the time we entered Washington, D.C., we were all a bit depressed because the next border was Virginia—back to segregation. But, once again, my parents were thoughtful and clever. They promised us that we would go back to New Jersey every summer for a week or two, and that gave us so much to look forward to. In fact, Lutrell and I applied the countdown game to months of the year. And every summer, after returning home from New Jersey, we would begin counting down the months to the next year's escape from the South.

These precious family vacations continued through 1965, the year I graduated from high school. And even though the Civil Rights Act had become law the previous year, the signs of segregation didn't disappear from the Southern states until around 1967, when I was 20 years old and entering my junior year in college. But, not surprisingly, as racial barriers were coming down, my parents never asked, "What took so long?" They said only, "Thank God we lived to see this!"

I use the word "remarkable" quite often in describing my parents, because that's what they were—simply remarkable. They were both born and raised in rural Charles City County, Virginia, and both came from large families—my dad was one of eleven children, my mother one of ten. They were teenagers in the early years of the Great Depression and both dropped out of high school so they could work and help support their families—a common occurrence among poor families at that time, and certainly among poor black families in the South. But even though their formal education was limited, my parents were smart and literate. They taught me to read when I was four years old, and placed a great value on education—not only as a path to building a career, but also as a means to a more enriching life.

My mom was a housewife, the common term for a homemaker in those days, and my dad was a laborer. He worked his entire adult life at the Newport News Shipbuilding & Dry Dock Company, commonly known as the shipyard. Newport News was slightly more than a one-hour drive from our home, so my parents got up at 4:00 a.m. every weekday. They would eat breakfast together, and then my dad would make the long drive to the shipyard. His work was manual labor in the truest sense—extremely physically demanding both in the oppressive heat of summer and bitter cold of winter, constantly lifting and carrying heavy objects. He would usually get home around 5:30 p.m., and even after a day of hard work and a long commute, he would find the time and energy to play baseball or basketball with his boys. By 6:30, we were usually ready for dinner. And, after we said a prayer over the meal, it was family time—engaging in conversation and lots of laughter. Most nights, as dinner was ending and homework was about to begin, my parents would remind Lutrell and me of the struggles they faced and how hard they had to work, and that a good education would enable us to have a better life.

The public school nearest to our house was within walking distance, less than a half mile away, but that was the white school. We were bussed three miles past that school every day to the black school, in compliance with segregation laws. Despite the common practice of states' providing more funding and better resources to white schools while neglecting black schools, my school was blessed with some amazing teachers. Great teachers can often compensate for poor funding and modest resources by making the learning experience exciting, and that is exactly what my teachers did. They encouraged and challenged me, stimulated my intellectual curiosity, and built on the foundation that my parents had established at home. I was acutely aware of the disparity between black schools and white schools and how the states had designed it that way, but I also knew that I was in a special place with a great community of support that would enable me to overcome the scars of discrimination.

Many of my schoolteachers left powerful and positive impressions on me, and three are especially memorable: Mrs. Montague, my third- and fourth-grade teacher; Mr. Johnson, my seventh-grade teacher; and, in high school, Mrs. Jefferson, who taught me algebra 1 and geometry.

Mrs. Montague was a no-nonsense, strict disciplinarian. When she asked a yes-or-no question, students were required to answer, "Yes, Mrs. Montague," or "No, Mrs. Montague." She insisted that we enunciate clearly and utter every syllable with clarity and precision. There was no mumbling or garbling of words in Mrs. Montague's class. She reminded us every day that presenting ourselves to the world in a dignified manner would make a positive impression and help open doors of opportunity. So, along with teaching us the "three Rs," Mrs. Montague emphasized communication techniques such as making eye contact, offering a firm handshake, maintaining straight and strong posture, and, of course, speaking proper English. There was not a single day that Mrs. Montague allowed our eight- and nine-year-old brains to forget that the outside world judged us harshly and defined us in a narrow, stereotypical way. But positive first impressions, she taught us, could shatter those stereotypes and encourage people to see our individual characteristics.

Despite the rigidity of Mrs. Montague's approach to teaching, it was always clear that she cared deeply about her students. I think she was a visionary—she wanted our generation of black youth to be equipped to compete for opportunities that her generation had been denied. So, her manner in the classroom was tough and demanding, even a bit scary sometimes, but she was never boring. Something about her intensity made her presentation of the subject matter fascinating. At the end of a day in Mrs. Montague's class, I felt inspired. I couldn't wait to get home and work on my assignments.

William Henry Johnson, Jr., was the first male teacher I ever had. Before I reached seventh grade, I used to hear the older kids talk about how much they loved Mr. Johnson. He could be tough, they said, but he was lively and entertaining, and he made the learning experience fun. They were right. Here was a guy who taught English, math, history, and world geography with equal mastery of the subjects, and he seemed to have so much fun doing his job that his students genuinely enjoyed being in his classroom.

Mr. Johnson was tall and athletic-looking, with a quick wit and a warm, infectious smile. And, although we certainly viewed him as a strong authority figure, he did not rule the classroom with fear and intimidation. Much to the contrary, his style was to engage us with just enough humor and playfulness to arouse our intellectual curiosity. And then, before we knew what was happening, we had actually learned something of value. He was a master of puns and wordplay, and he exuded sheer joy in awakening our young, fertile minds. As a result, even students who were not highly motivated achievers experienced the joy of learning in his classes. Mr. Johnson was arguably the coolest teacher ever.

One of the proudest moments in my life was having the chance to recognize Mr. Johnson publicly on the airwaves of a 50,000-watt radio station in Richmond. Here's how that came about. Former Virginia governor Doug Wilder, who in 1989 became the first black elected governor in US history, was a friend of mine. Governor Wilder was hosting a talk show on Richmond's WRVA, a powerhouse radio station on the East Coast. He contacted me at *GMA* and invited me to be a guest on his show for National Teacher Day. Since I was a prominent native Virginian, he wanted my reflections on a favorite teacher who had helped shape my direction in life. Of course, I quickly blurted out Mr. Johnson's name as I accepted the governor's invitation. Much to my surprise, on the day of the broadcast, when WRVA called me at my *GMA* number in New York, Mr. Johnson was on the line with us from his home in Richmond. He was battling cancer at that time, and as I struggled to fight back the tears, I paid tribute to Mr. Johnson as perhaps the finest teacher a student could ever have. When God created Mr. Johnson, He threw away the teacher's mold. It was a touching and memorable moment for me and, I presume, for Mr. Johnson. I am deeply grateful for the opportunity that I had to thank and recognize this extraordinary man in such a public way. He was more than deserving.

And that brings us to Mrs. Jefferson. She and Mr. Johnson had many similar traits. They were both brilliant in their command of so many subjects, and both brought a touch of humor and likeability to the classroom that made their demands for excellence and accountability seem attainable. Mrs. Jefferson taught several math courses; she was my teacher for algebra 1 in the eighth grade, and again for plane geometry in the tenth grade. Now, bear in mind that for many students, algebra was the equivalent in mathematics of Shakespeare in English. Many students were tuned out before the course even began. Yet, Mrs. Jefferson made algebra not only approachable, but also logical and interesting. Those equations made sense. Or, to put it another way, it all added up!

Mrs. Jefferson welcomed one-on-one discussions with students after class, and she often stayed after the school day had ended, delaying her nearly one-hour drive home to

Williamsburg in order to give individual students the extra encouragement and confidence they needed to tackle their homework assignments. Her dedication to helping us master the information necessary for advancement to the next level was remarkable. Mrs. Jefferson cultivated such a passion in me for algebra and geometry that I initially chose mathematics as my major when I entered college.

One of my sweetest memories of Mrs. Jefferson was her insatiable appetite for celebrity news. I would often linger after class had ended so she and I could thumb through the popular Hollywood gossip magazines of that era (circa 1960) to find out who was marrying whom and who was rumored to be cheating on whom. Mrs. Jefferson was a great teacher and mentor and—within the context of the teacher-student relationship—a dear friend.

Throughout my childhood, I never doubted that a world of opportunity would be open to me. I was confident that I could achieve whatever I dreamed. And this "audacity of hope" was clearly the result of my parents' unconditional love, support, and positive reinforcement. They encouraged me to be an achiever, to strive for excellence, and to be ultra-prepared for the opportunities that would surely come my way. They also placed great importance on character values—integrity, humility, devotion to family. And, perhaps above all, my parents taught me that life has meaning—that life is a gift from God, and I should honor Him by living a purposeful life.

These foundational teachings were the guiding force that carried me into my adult years. Within a year after receiving my B.A. degree in English from Hampton Institute (now Hampton University), I had married Diane and begun my career in TV. I started as a news reporter for WWBT-TV, Channel 12, the NBC station in Richmond. This was 1971—in the capital of the Confederacy—and I was delivering the evening news to an audience of people with whom I could not have shared a public restroom, water fountain, or space at a lunch counter just five years earlier. I was only the third person of color to hold such a position in the Richmond TV market, yet I felt that I belonged. Not only had the world changed, as my parents had said it would, but the change felt comfortable and natural to me. Those days of Jim Crow segregation, of in-your-face racism, had not faded from my memory. After all, resistance to desegregation in the South was ongoing; it was mean and ugly, and often violent. But my positive outlook would not be dimmed. Painful memories lingered, but the road ahead seemed bright.

✳   ✳   ✳

I could not have dreamed of a more encouraging start to a career than I had in Richmond. Doug Hill, Channel 12's news director and the man who hired me, reminded me of the Lou Grant character in *The Mary Tyler Moore Show*. Like Lou, Doug seemed rough and rugged on the outside, but inside had a big, soft heart and an unparalleled sense of fairness and integrity. He was also the first news director in Richmond to hire a person of color in an on-air position, which resulted in his receiving death threats. If I had to point to someone as a mentor in my early years, it would be Doug Hill. He showed confidence in my talent and judgment right away, encouraged me to be myself—transparent, even vulnerable—on the air, and offered tough-love critiques when necessary. Largely because of Doug's support, I learned to feel at ease on camera very quickly, and that fueled my growth as a journalist and TV personality.

During my first year at Channel 12, I was strictly a news reporter. I covered state and local politics, general assignment stories, and occasionally stumbled onto a heartwarming human-interest story. But during my second year on the air, something happened that would change the trajectory of my career in the most amazing fashion. Our longtime weatherman resigned on short notice, and Doug asked me to fill in for two weeks while the station searched for a new weatherperson. Having done a lot of science reporting, I knew quite a bit about the atmosphere, the jet stream, and how air masses interact, so I could talk knowledgeably about basic weather phenomena. But the mechanics of presenting weather on the air—describing symbols on the map and properly addressing the camera—were new and challenging to me. Doug took me under his wing and gave me some coaching, and, by the end of my two weeks of filling in, I was quite comfortable in the role.

Next came the big surprise. The station's general manager called me to his office and said that during my fill-in period, I had become a hit and our ratings had gone up. He offered me the full-time weather position. I was flattered but also hesitant to accept, since I thought of myself as a journalist—a serious news reporter. However, once I was assured that I could continue covering my political beat, I embraced my new assignment, an opportunity that became the springboard for a career that has far exceeded my early dreams.

One of the most rewarding things about this exciting time in my life was that my childhood home was only 25 miles from Richmond, and my parents could watch their son on the news every night! No words can describe the joy they felt. They had invested a lifetime of hard work, sacrifice, patience, and prayer in the hope that their children would live in a world of equal opportunity and racial justice. And now they were reaping the rewards of their investment—rewards beyond anything they had dared to dream. They felt so thankful, so proud, so fulfilled, and I felt thankful, too—thankful that they lived to see this day of prayers answered.

How is it, then, that I could have fallen prey to something so antithetical to my parents' teachings—something so ungodly, if you will—as compulsive gambling?

That question haunted me as I went through the ordeal of my 1984 bankruptcy and the loss of my home. I didn't have the heart—or courage—to tell my parents that my tax and financial problems were the result of excessive gambling, so I carefully crafted an explanation for them of how heartless the IRS can be. I couldn't claim that I was a victim of racism, because the IRS examiner in charge of my case was also black. I could, however, convince anyone who would listen of the viciousness of the taxman. After all, hasn't everyone heard stories about the merciless collection tactics of the Internal Revenue Service? I refused to let my parents suffer the devastation of learning how foolish and wasteful I had been. But, of course, I was protecting not only my parents but my own foolish pride as well.

* * *

Following the bankruptcy settlement, I took a brief break from gambling—a break that lasted not quite a year. It was 1985. Jason was ten and Jessica was seven. I had resettled my family in a nice house, which we were renting with the option to buy. It was only a short distance from where we had previously lived, so my kids remained in the same school and we were essentially in the same community with all the familiar shops, restaurants, and friends we had known for years.

As the pain of the previous year began to ease, I was eager to return to the high-roller lifestyle. Remember, in the broader picture of things, my gambling was part of a glamorous and exciting social experience. The casino-hotels that hosted my visits would provide transportation—limos to Atlantic City, first-class airfare to Las Vegas—plus a luxurious suite for my family or two couples, meals at the finest gourmet restaurants, and tickets to headliner shows and major sports events. So, I usually had family and/or friends with me on these trips. In fact, most family vacations in the western US included a three-day stop in Las Vegas on the way home. When the dinners and entertainment ended, Diane and the kids would go to bed, and I would spend most of the night in the casino.

Diane certainly wasn't thrilled about my return to gambling, but once again, consider the context. I would suggest that we go down to Atlantic City with another couple for a weekend so we could see Diana Ross or Frank Sinatra, Buddy Hackett or Rodney Dangerfield. And we could dine at one of our favorite gourmet restaurants while sipping from bottles of rare, old-vintage Bordeaux wine. Not only would all expenses be comped by the casino, but the spouses of high rollers were often given shopping sprees worth thousands of dollars in the elegant, upscale shops, which were present in all the major casino-hotels. Of course, during the afternoon hours before our dinners and shows, I would be doing battle with the casino. And at the end of the evening when everyone else was ready for bed, I would return to the casino for some late-night recreation.

In those early days after my yearlong layoff from gambling, I probably didn't show signs of compulsion or desperate eagerness to rush off to the casino after dinner or a show, but I would often place my hand to my ear and say jokingly to my family and friends, "I hear the tables calling my name." Understanding, of course, that I was referring to the blackjack tables, or the craps tables, or whatever casino game I had in mind, they would usually just laugh and wish me good luck. And, as chance would have it, luck was my companion in the early stages of my return to gambling—which made it so easy for me to get sucked in again.

When the first few trips to Vegas and Atlantic City after my gambling hiatus padded my pockets with a few thousand dollars, I felt a strange mix of excitement and guilt. I was happy to be on this little winning streak, but I felt like I had come into "dirty" money. I tried to relieve my guilt by doing something useful or responsible with my winnings. I bought my parents a new car, treated my family to a vacation, put some money in the stock market, and gave more generously when the donation plate was passed around at church. Soon, the guilt began to ease, but at about the same time, my luck began to turn sour.

About six months after my return to the casino wars, I was losing again. Trips to Atlantic City were becoming more frequent. Excuses to visit Las Vegas were more carefully crafted.

I was drifting back into dark and familiar territory. But then life delivered another stunning surprise.

Amazing grace paved me a path out of the darkness. The ABC network program *Good Morning America* offered me a full-time position as one of its three principal "family members." This was early summer, 1986, just a year and a half after my bankruptcy and the loss of my home, and I was being invited to move up from the local news to the national stage. What an amazing career opportunity! And what a blessing for me and my family! Surely this was just the fresh start I needed to help me turn my life around.

But addicts don't usually handle sharp turns very well.

Chapter Four

I spent twelve and a half glorious years at *Good Morning America*. David Hartman and Joan Lunden were the co-hosts when I joined the team in July 1986. Shortly thereafter, in early 1987, Charlie Gibson succeeded David as the male co-host, and I was part of America's three-member morning-TV family with Charlie and Joan for most of my remaining years at *GMA*. The bond we formed on that program was one of profound friendship and genuine affection. And that apparently came across to viewers, as *GMA* soared to number one in the morning ratings during the late '80s and early '90s, when millions of Americans embraced us as their TV family.

My primary area of reporting at *GMA* was national weather, which meant much more than standing in front of a map of the 48 contiguous states. I also reported on location from numerous hurricanes, floods, blizzards, fires, earthquakes, and virtually every imaginable natural disaster. These were always challenging, and sometimes dangerous, assignments, but they gave me a great opportunity to exercise my journalistic skills. Most mornings in the studio, I was the fun-loving, quick-witted weatherman. But on these serious assignments I was a journalist—a source of vital information, and often a voice of comfort and reassurance.

From the very beginning of my stint on *GMA,* I was given the opportunity to do so much more than forecast the weather. It was an incredible experience! I reported from major sports events that included the Olympics, Super Bowls, World Series, the Indianapolis 500, championship boxing matches, and more. I was the program's goodwill ambassador and traveled to all 50 states, doing live remotes at countless festivals, parades, county fairs, cook-offs, hot-air-balloon events, circuses, carnivals, Oktoberfests, rodeos—as many varied events and venues as our producers could dream up.

I also had the tremendous honor of serving as the ABC television network's spokesperson for literacy for many years. In this role I visited schools and read to students. I appeared at promotional events on behalf of the network, sharing my passion for literacy and describing my early fascination with books. And, during the years when First Lady Barbara Bush was a champion of literacy, I was invited to broadcast live from the White House, joining her in reading storybooks to young children. As a bonus, I got to meet and briefly interview President George H. W. Bush.

That visit to the Bush 41 White House was not my first— nor was it my only—encounter with a US president. During the years that followed, I met and/or interviewed former presidents Nixon, Ford, and Carter, and future presidents Obama and Trump—but those stories will come later. The point here is that my time at *Good Morning America* was the richest and most rewarding professional experience I could have dreamed of—beyond any dreams, in fact. It also enabled me to provide a measure of security for my family that I could never have imagined at the beginning of my career. Yet, I used this wonderful opportunity, this dream job, to enable something else as well—my gambling habit.

It was no secret among my colleagues at *GMA* that I loved to visit the casinos and enjoyed the high-roller treatment. Yet, I doubt that any of them realized the seriousness of my addiction. Because I was on a live remote nearly every Friday, traveling all over the country, I would generally leave our studio right after the broadcast on Thursday—along with a field producer and a technical coordinator—to fly out to my Friday-morning-broadcast destination. Then, following my final segment on Friday, instead of returning to New York I would often change my company-issued ticket and fly to either Las Vegas (if I happened to be west of the Mississippi River) or Atlantic City (if east of the Mississippi), and return home on Saturday. On some occasions, I persuaded my colleagues to go with me and treated them to a slice of the high-roller lifestyle. They would get to stay in my luxury suite, dine with me at the finest and fanciest restaurants, and enjoy all the other perks and privileges that came my way. This became such a regular feature of "travels with Spencer" that producers and other staff members actually competed for the opportunity to go on remotes with me.

As my earnings and my prominence on national TV increased, so did my gambling losses. By the early 1990s, I had opened and exhausted lines of credit at as many as 14 casinos, counting both Las Vegas and Atlantic City. Also by this time, the thrill of gambling had faded considerably. I was now frequenting the casinos not just for fun and excitement, but out of desperation—trying to keep my financial house of cards from collapsing. Here's how that game worked. Generally, when you sign a credit marker during a casino visit, if it is not paid after

30 days, that marker is deposited like a check at your bank. And if that marker bounces, the "returned check" is reported across a worldwide network of gambling establishments, all outstanding markers at all casinos immediately become due, and your consumer credit score is shattered.

So, here I was satisfactorily meeting the normal, real-life obligations of a mortgage, private-school tuition, and plain old family fun while feeling terrified by this dangerous balancing act of floating my casino debt. After years of staggering gambling losses, I was continually faced with outstanding markers at various casinos becoming due for deposit and not having sufficient funds to cover the items. My years-long way of dealing with this was absolutely exhausting, physically and emotionally. I would go to one of the few casinos where I had a paid-up credit line, claim a spot at a craps or blackjack table, and sign a marker for my maximum amount of available credit. I would then kill enough time making modest bets to give the appearance of having actually gambled, before beginning the ordeal of trying to cash in my chips. Cashing in thousands of dollars in chips when you have an outstanding marker is difficult. Those whose job it is to monitor your play at the tables are fully aware when you walk away without having given much "action," so cashing in $9,000 worth of chips when you've just signed a $10,000 marker is no easy feat. It requires playing the incremental game—cashing in $1,100 here and $1,300 there—and it's time-consuming.

Once the task of cashing in was completed, I would take the cash to Casino X, pay off my nearly overdue markers there, play the same "cashing in" game, and then proceed to Casinos Y and Z. This was usually an all-day or all-night ordeal, but it would buy me another 30 days before I had to repeat the performance—at least at those three casinos. There were always others that would demand my presence in the next week or two.

By the time I reached this point in my addiction, I had become supremely skilled at borrowing money. I'm not proud of that, but it's what I felt I had to do in order to avoid losing face. I was certainly not going to let anything get in the way of taking care of my family. So, when gambling losses mounted, I would increase the mortgage on my house and pay down my casino debt. Or, I would increase the credit limits on my ordinary consumer lines of credit. But I could not find the courage or the will to confront the casinos and try to arrange a payoff plan. I had tried that a couple of times in years past. On both occasions they were tougher to bargain with than the IRS, and they filed judgments against me. Therefore, I couldn't take the risk of trying to settle with ten or twelve casino collections agents, knowing that they would ruin my "real life" credit rating and that the publicity would likely damage my career.

The stress was overwhelming. I was often unable to sleep at night. Yet, I somehow continued getting up at 3:30 a.m. to go to work with a smile on my face and with genuine enthusiasm for my job. And I came home every afternoon—when I wasn't traveling—excited to have dinner with my wife and kids, hear the latest school stories, and watch our favorite nighttime sitcoms. My family knew that I was managing a lot of debt, and they certainly knew that I gambled excessively. Now that my kids were teenagers and too smart to be fooled, I began explaining why I had to do this juggling act at the casinos and why my "real life" debts were greater than my ability to simply pay them off and retire them.

Thankfully, I had some very good banking relationships. Mortgage refinances and credit-limit increases were not a big problem, because my income was substantial and my payment history was outstanding. I was often surprised, however, that my primary lenders didn't probe further into why a person with my high earnings was in constant debt and in need of frequent debt consolidation. I never disclosed the gambling, of course, nor did I ever file a fraudulent credit application. But I did know how to highlight those credit-worthy factors that would gain the most favorable view of a prospective lender. I had mastered the game so well that I was playing it to my own detriment.

* * *

Getting back to the concern that gambling might cause me great public embarrassment or cost me my job, there was one event that I believe planted suspicion in the minds of one or two ABC executives, and this made me more fearful and anxious than I had ever been in the face of the hurricanes, floods, or earthquakes I had experienced. It occurred in January 1996, but let me provide some context before sharing the story.

For five consecutive years, beginning in 1991, *GMA* had sent me to Las Vegas to report from CES, the Consumer Electronics Show, which opens every year on the first Friday in January. This global electronics and consumer technology trade show is the largest of its kind in the world, and for several years my son, Jason, had asked if he could accompany me. Jason was not a little kid anymore. He was a few weeks away from turning 21 and fascinated with innovations in technology, especially in audio-video devices. So, I made plans to take him with me to the CES that was to open on January 5, 1996. I even bought him a first-class ticket so he could fly with me, since *GMA* always provided me with first-class air travel on my road trips. Well, much to my surprise and dismay, I was told just a few days before Jason and I were scheduled to depart—and after I had paid for his ticket—that *GMA* was not sending me to that year's CES. Instead, a well-known technology reporter was given the assignment. *What?*

After recovering from my initial surprise and disappointment, I realized that since the show was opening on Friday, Jason and I could still fly out to Vegas right after my *GMA* broadcast Friday morning. We would arrive by noon Vegas time and still have the rest of the day and most of the weekend to check out all the latest gadgets. Plus, I could do a little gambling and enjoy a couple of gourmet meals with my son. So, in the absence of travel provided by *GMA*, I simply redeemed some of my frequent-flyer miles for a first-class ticket, and Jason and I were off to Vegas for the opening of CES.

We had an awesome day on Friday. Jason was like a little kid as we roamed the convention center floor examining one dazzling new bit of technology after the other. And after an extraordinary dining experience that night, I actually spent only a limited amount of time gambling and went to bed early enough to get what qualifies as a full night's sleep in Las Vegas.

When I woke up Saturday morning, I turned on the TV and heard the shocking news that a dangerous blizzard was about to hit the northeastern US. Snow was expected to begin falling that afternoon on the eastern seaboard—it was already snowing in the Upper Midwest—and airports across the entire northeastern quadrant of the country were closing and might not reopen until Monday or Tuesday. How had this storm developed so fast? There had been no indication of a blizzard in the observations I used to compile my forecast for the previous day's broadcast on *GMA*. What had happened? I was in panic mode. My heart was pounding and my stomach was churning. If I were to be stranded in Las Vegas, of all places, and unable to get back to New York for Monday morning's coverage of such a major weather event, I feared that I would be in *big* trouble. Would anyone who knew me actually believe that I just happened to be stranded in Las Vegas while a major blizzard was paralyzing half of the country?

I spent the next hour frantically calling airlines, trying to find some way to get back to New York. There was no way. Airports from Boston to Atlanta were closing, and all weekend flights were cancelled. For the first time in my career, I seriously feared that I might lose my job. *GMA* had a relatively new executive producer at that time. He and I had a very limited history together, and I had no idea what he knew or how he felt about my "habit." I only knew that I could not afford to be stuck in Las Vegas and absent from work while a historic storm was the dominant national news story.

I called his home number and got his voicemail. I left a sorrowful message, explaining my desperate attempts to find some way back to New York. I asked if he wanted me to travel to some other location in order to be on the air Monday morning but *not* in Las Vegas. How about St. Louis, Chicago, Memphis? Anyplace where planes were flying, so I could at least be on the air on Monday. When an hour had passed and I had not heard from him, I called a second time and once again got his voicemail. I left a second message, again trying to convey how seriously I was trying to get out of Las Vegas and at least head in the direction of New York. Another hour or more went by, with no call back. Finally, on my third attempt, he answered. The tone of his voice felt more damning to me than the few words he uttered. Without ever saying that he didn't believe my story, he made it very clear that he was deeply disturbed by this situation. And he stated the obvious—it would seem very odd for *GMA*'s weatherman, the reporter who had covered every natural calamity for ABC over the past decade, to be absent from the broadcast on a day when a storm of biblical proportions dominated national news.

I walked around like a zombie for the remainder of that weekend. All I could do was hope and pray that this event would not be a career-ender for me. New York–area airports reopened on Monday. Jason and I arrived at home near the end of the day. When I returned to work on Tuesday, I was greeted with an air of relative normalcy. No one in management ever uttered a word to me about my absence on the day of Stormageddon. During the remaining three years on my contract, I was treated as respectfully and featured as prominently as ever on *GMA*. But for many long months, I had a haunting and lingering fear that this incident may have created doubts at the highest executive levels about my reliability. It should have created doubt in me as well about whether my career, reputation, and family could survive the dangerous path I was traveling.

Chapter Five

The 1996 Stormageddon experience should have been the wake-up call I needed. The fear of losing everything I had worked to build over the years—family, career, reputation—should have shocked some sense into me. But rational decision-making does not come easily to an addict, and I was not yet willing to acknowledge and confront my addiction.

I've heard numerous psychologists and recovering addicts say that an addict often needs to hit rock bottom or become "broken" before making a serious effort to end the addictive behavior. It took me many years to reach that point, probably because I had so many extraordinarily positive things happening in my life at the same time as I was indulging my addiction. I wasn't close enough to feeling broken.

Even with the ongoing financial worries, I found great joy in my personal life. Family time was my favorite time. I looked forward to the simple everyday pleasures like watching TV together or sharing what happened at work or school over dinner. Vacations were always fun and exciting, even the ones that included a stopover in Las Vegas on the way home.

We planned several family vacations around some of my *Good Morning America* travel destinations, one of the most memorable of which was Sweden. *GMA* was doing a week of daily broadcasts there, giving our viewers what we called a vicarious vacation. Our program was also broadcast on Sveriges Television, Sweden's public TV broadcaster, each day. On the very first show, I announced that I had a bit of Scandinavian ancestry, so for the rest of the week, I wanted to be known by the popular Swedish name Sven. Well, our show drew a loyal audience of Swedish viewers, and I became widely and immediately recognized. Everywhere we went that week—major cities, small towns, wherever—Swedes greeted me like I was a rock star. "Sven, how's it going?" "Sven, may I take a picture with you?" "Sven, I love your tan!"

I was so captivated by the warm embrace of the people and the stunning beauty of the country that I asked my boss (Phil Beuth, the greatest TV executive I've ever known) if I could remain in Sweden for another week after we finished our assignment, because I wanted to bring my family over for a little vacation. He gave me the okay, so I called Diane and had her and the kids fly over to Stockholm the very next day. Jason and Jessica were 13 and 10, respectively, yet they still talk about that amazing vacation nearly 30 years later.

Not only was I happy and fulfilled by my routine family life, but I was also able to provide my family with memorable special experiences that we will treasure forever. The pure joy that I derived from family time gave me comfort and reassurance when I was stressed out over financial pressures. Smiling faces at dinner, welcome-home hugs at the end of a workday, bedtime prayers—these precious gifts gave my life meaning, made me feel loved and valued, and kept me from going crazy when gambling had dragged me to that very scary place at the edge of sanity.

*   *   *

Just as my family life was a source of joy and stability, so too was my professional life. Consider this: during my years at *GMA*, only the three major networks—ABC, NBC, and CBS—had programs like ours, and each show featured just three primary people. Essentially, that means only nine people on the planet were fortunate enough to have such a wonderfully fulfilling job as I had at *GMA*. For that I am forever grateful. My assignments, from lighthearted features to hard news, took me to all 50 states in the US and across four continents. Yet, as exciting and enriching as the travel assignments were, the daily in-studio broadcasts were just as thrilling.

This was a two-hour news and entertainment program that gave me the opportunity to meet and interview the most prominent people in the world from the fields of politics, sports, entertainment, the arts, medicine, space exploration, education, technology, and more. Presidents, monarchs, championship athletes, Nobel Prize recipients, Oscar winners, authors, rock stars—they all appeared on *GMA*. And interestingly enough, some of the most memorable people I met and reported on were not necessarily famous, but just ordinary people who had done something extraordinary in their lives.

Some assignments and personal encounters have left indelible memories—experiences I could have had only in my job at *GMA*. As you read these stories, bear in mind something I said in an earlier chapter—many famous people who were guests on the show were also regular *GMA* viewers, and they were often as excited to meet us (the hosts) as we were to meet them.

Weather Duets

Guests who were waiting to be interviewed were often fascinated as they watched me do the weather. This was primarily because I was standing in front of a blank green wall, seemingly pointing to nothing, while the on-air image displayed various maps and graphics behind me. I not only took time during commercial breaks to demonstrate how this all worked, but also began the practice of inviting many of our celebrity guests to join me for live "weather duets," in which I would describe the weather conditions as they tried to point to the right spots that corresponded to what I was describing. Tom Hanks, Bill Murray, Chevy Chase, Billy Crystal, Henry Kissinger, Dionne Warwick, and Wynona Ryder make up just a short list of those who joined me in weather duets.

Some of them were actually pretty smooth, others were hilariously awkward, and all were entertaining. Arguably the most memorable duet was with Bill Murray. This occurred at least one year before he starred in the movie *Groundhog Day*, in which he played a TV weatherman. Bill was on *GMA* to promote an earlier film venture and seemed absolutely mesmerized as he watched me performing in front of the green screen, so I invited him to join me for my next segment. He happily said, "Okay," and what followed was one of the funniest two-minute segments ever on *GMA*.

About a year later, his film *Groundhog Day* was about to be released, and Bill was doing a promotional appearance on *The Today Show*, *GMA*'s top competitor. During his interview, Bill was asked by longtime *Today Show* weatherman Willard Scott, "What national TV weatherman did you study as you prepared for this role?" Bill replied, "Spencer Christian!" When someone at ABC played that clip for me, I almost fell off my chair with laughter. Of course, at the same time, I was immensely flattered.

Duke Snider

I was a huge baseball fan by the time I was four years old, and my favorite team was the Brooklyn Dodgers. My favorite player and childhood hero was Dodger center fielder and Hall of Famer Duke Snider. In the early to mid-1990s, Snider appeared as a guest on *GMA*. I was not scheduled to be part of that segment, so I decided to go to the green room, where guests wait before their scheduled appearances, and meet my boyhood idol. I can't begin to describe how nervous I was. What would I say? How would I introduce myself? What kind of mood would he be in? After all, guests usually began arriving at the studio by 6:00 a.m., so they weren't always happy and perky.

I finally gathered up my courage and entered the green room. There he was, "The Duke," as he was known—tall, silver-haired, and regal-looking—nearly 70 years old but with a strong, youthful bearing and a twinkle in his eye. As I approached him, before I could utter a word, he exclaimed, "Spencer, I was hoping to meet you. You're my favorite!" I was unable to speak coherently. He gave me a big bear hug and I wept as I told him he was my childhood hero. I literally had tears streaming down my cheeks as I tried to explain what a thrill it was to meet him. And then, as I went on and on describing some of his heroic moments from the 1950s that seemed almost like yesterday to me, The Duke became teary-eyed. For me, it was one of those once-in-a-lifetime moments that seemed too good to be true. Here I was telling my childhood hero how much I admired him, while he was telling me that he watched me regularly on

GMA and was excited to meet me! In what other job could that have happened?

Sidney Poitier

Can you think of any actor more gifted or dignified than Sidney Poitier? Actor, director, author, and diplomat, Sir Sidney Poitier is a man of immeasurable talent. He is also a trailblazer, the first African American to win an Academy Award for Best Actor, for his role in *Lilies of the Field* in 1964. He also gave highly acclaimed performances in *A Raisin in the Sun*; *To Sir, with Love*; *In the Heat of the Night*; *Guess Who's Coming to Dinner*; and many others.

I had a brief but personally meaningful encounter with Sir Sidney in 1997. *GMA* sent me on a remote to Richmond, Virginia, where my career had begun in 1971. After checking in at the historic Hotel Jefferson, I waited for the elevator on the hotel's second floor. As the door opened and I entered the rather crowded elevator, I couldn't help noticing that Sidney Poitier was on board, near the rear of the crowd. I entered and said nothing as I stared straight ahead while the doors closed. On the way up, the elevator stopped at the next floor, where everyone got off except Sir Sidney and me. Apparently, we were both going up to higher floors. As the doors closed again, Mr. Poitier said in that distinctive voice of his, "Mr. Christian, I am a great admirer of your work." I could not believe my ears! "You're an admirer of *my* work?" I said in disbelief. "I am a longtime admirer of *your* work. I am honored to meet you, and humbled by your gracious compliment." He smiled, shook my hand vigorously, and got off at the elevator's next stop. Now, left alone on the elevator, I wondered whether I had been coherent enough, eloquent enough, gracious enough to have even warranted sharing a brief conversation with Sir Sidney Poitier. I was pretty much in awe.

Once again, my broad exposure on *GMA* had made me recognizable to and admired by someone whose fame and accomplishments far exceeded mine.

Hugging the Queen

During my weeklong assignment in Sweden, I had the great pleasure of reporting from locations all over the country, while co-hosts Charlie Gibson and Joan Lunden were based solely in Stockholm every day. As a result, there were several distinguished Swedes interviewed by Charlie and Joan whom I did not get to meet. About a year after our amazing Swedish adventure, Sweden's Queen Sylvia came to visit the *GMA* studio in New York. As she and a cadre of photojournalists waited at the studio entrance, one of our producers came to tell me that Queen Sylvia wanted to meet "Sven." I left my dressing room and hurried over to meet the queen. As I approached her, she extended her hand to shake mine and asked if I would pose for some pictures with her. I felt honored.

Now, bear in mind that I am frequently invited to take pictures with people, and I'm accustomed to putting my arm around the other person's shoulder as we pose. So, without thinking about the protocol of not casually touching royalty, I placed my arm around Queen Sylvia's shoulder. Suddenly, an audible gasp arose from the photographers. Realizing what I had done, I sheepishly pulled my arm back. But, immediately soothing my embarrassment, Queen Sylvia said, "It is okay for you, Sven." So, I put my arm around her shoulder again, and the room was aglow with flashes from the cameras. We all had a hearty laugh, and I'm guessing those pictures were widely distributed in the Scandinavian press. Being "Sven" does have its privileges!

Ali and Me

Muhammad Ali was for many years considered the most famous person on the planet. His name was known and his face recognized in every corner of the world. And I had the indescribable joy of getting to know him as a friend.

We first met in 1980, before the effects of his Parkinson's disease became noticeable, and before I joined *GMA* full-time. My primary role at that time was hosting *Good Morning New York*, which aired immediately after *GMA* on WABC-TV. Ali's then wife, Veronica, a former model, was a frequent guest on the show, doing segments on beauty and fashion. Ali accompanied Veronica for her first appearance and invited me to join them for lunch after the show. Of course, I said yes, and we became fast friends.

Getting to the restaurant was a challenge, even though it was only three blocks from the studio. Ali attracted a crowd—big-time! I've been in the company of some very famous people, but I have never met anyone else with the charisma, the sheer magnetism, of Muhammad Ali. We had walked only about a block and a half when we were mobbed by more than fifty people tearing at Ali and screaming his name. It was scary.

While at lunch, Ali asked me if I ever took my kids to the movies, to Disney World, or to a local park to play ball. I said, "Yes, of course." He said with a tone of sadness, "I can't do that. I have to rent a theater if I want to see a movie with my kids or pay for a private facility to have play time." It was clear, from the mob scene we had just escaped, what he was talking about. He was a prisoner of his own celebrity. He couldn't enjoy a normal life.

At one point, as we began to bond, in a gesture of almost childlike playfulness Ali flashed a smile as bright as the morning sun, playfully shook his fist under my nose, and said, "I can't let my wife spend too much time around you, because you're one of them pretty n--gers." Now, this is not a word that I use, but Ali meant it in the most innocent, flattering, and familial way. So, I took that as a compliment and we had a big laugh. In fact, that was an especially fine compliment coming from the self-proclaimed "prettiest fighter of all time."

Over the years, even during his physical decline, I interviewed Ali on numerous occasions and hung out with him at various social functions and celebrity events. And every single time I saw him, even when his speech was reduced to a mumble, he gave me a big hug and whispered, "You're still pretty." In addition to those lighter moments, we also shared stories about our respective experiences growing up in the Jim Crow South—he in Kentucky and I in Virginia. Ali had achieved fame and fortune with his remarkable boxing talent, along with his dazzling wit and charm. And he wasn't kidding around when proclaimed throughout his career, "I am the greatest!" Yet, he looked up to black professionals who had "made it" because of their polish and education. He often cited Bryant Gumbel and me as people he admired and respected.

On my final broadcast at *GMA*, December 22, 1998, as my colleagues were giving me going-away gifts, Charlie Gibson unveiled a gift from Muhammad Ali. It was a nearly life-sized portrait of him, on which he had written these words: "To Spencer, You're the Greatest." I melted right there on national TV. Tears flowed down my cheeks. That portrait of Ali is prominently displayed on a wall in my home, and it's one of my most treasured possessions.

Hurricanes

While most of my *GMA* assignments posed no threat to my safety or physical well-being, there was clearly an element of danger in my on-location coverage of catastrophic events such as devastating floods, crippling blizzards, massive wildfires, powerful earthquakes, and no fewer than twelve hurricanes. In fact, early in my stint at *GMA*, staff members began referring to me as "the Master of Disaster." The nickname made me proud, but earning that title meant placing myself in harm's way on numerous occasions.

My hurricane assignments were among the most dramatic and visually compelling. During my live reports, I was usually wearing protective goggles and heavy raingear while clinging tightly with one arm to a utility pole or another stationary object, sometimes leaning into a powerful 90-mile-per-hour wind gust. Pelted by horizontal rain and flying debris, I had to yell into my microphone to be heard over the howling storm. This is what producers call "good TV." I had other names for it.

If you know much about the massive size and force of a hurricane, you might wonder how in the world reporters and their crews get to the assigned locations. After all, when even a minimal hurricane is expected to make landfall, airports within a 100-mile radius or greater begin shutting down. When I was sent to cover Hurricane Bertha, for example, in July of 1996, my itinerary had to factor in that the storm was expected to first hit land just south of coastal Wilmington, North Carolina, but its turbulence could potentially be felt from northern Florida to central New Jersey. That's more than half of the country's Atlantic coastline. As coastal cities began announcing airport closures and possible evacuations, I was ticketed to fly from New York to Charlotte, North Carolina, which is well inland, the day before Bertha's expected arrival, and drive a rental car to Wilmington. Once there, I would hope for weather conditions that were "dramatic and visually compelling" for the next morning's broadcast.

In addition to the logistical challenges of getting to broadcast destinations for hurricane reporting, there was also the issue of preparedness. Knowing that hurricanes typically cause widespread flooding and power outages, my crew and I would often find ourselves stranded for two days or longer in a flood-ravaged town with no electricity, hot water, safe drinking water, or open restaurants—thus, no access to freshly prepared food—and sometimes no clear idea of when or how we would get home.

On the Hurricane Bertha assignment, my crew and I stopped at a grocery store on the drive from Charlotte to Wilmington. We stocked up on bottled water, nonperishable food items (chips, nuts, bread, peanut butter, and so on), flashlights and batteries, and first-aid supplies. When we arrived at our downtown Wilmington hotel in the late afternoon the day before our *GMA* broadcast, the skies were already looking dark and dreary. Local businesses were shutting down, and large numbers of people were evacuating—moving farther inland, where the storm would be less damaging. Bertha was closing in on the North Carolina coast and was expected to hit land the following morning near Wrightsville Beach. When *GMA* signed on the air at 7:00 a.m. the next day, I was on the beach in full hurricane-coverage mode. When Charlie and Joan tossed the broadcast from the studio to me, the scene was dramatic. I was being pounded by wind and rain and sand, with the roar of the storm overriding the sound of my voice. The producers back in New York had the "good TV" they had hoped for.

Bertha's full force had not yet arrived when I got off the air at 9:00 a.m., so my crew and I were able to scurry safely back to our hotel. Just before noon, it seemed like all hell was breaking loose. Bertha moved onshore packing sustained winds of nearly 100 miles per hour and gusts over 115 miles per hour. The storm surge at the coast was up to 10 feet high. Meanwhile, I was hunkered down in a ground-level hotel banquet room with no windows in order to avoid being hit by shattered glass. Even on the ground floor we could feel the building sway from the force of the wind. My cameraman had not been in a storm like this before, so I tried to reassure him by explaining that we were in a relatively safe spot, in a very sturdy and stable structure. And, since hurricane winds diminish as the storm moves over land, we were not likely to see death and destruction at our location away from the coastline.

By midafternoon, Bertha had moved north of Wilmington and we were feeling much safer. However, coastal towns had been devastated, and much of the eastern half of the state had suffered widespread flooding and destruction of property. Damage estimates were in the tens of millions of dollars. My crew and I spent one more night without lights, running water, or a hot meal. The next day, we drove to Charlotte and boarded a flight back to New York. Bertha had made a sharp turn out to sea, but had left her mark for hundreds of miles up and down the Atlantic coast.

I was in many other hurricanes over the years—with names like Hugo, Gilbert, Fran, Opal, Georges (the French way), Floyd—but Bertha was one of only a few whose timing was in sync with our broadcast schedule and delivered the dramatic on-air punch that resulted in "good TV."

Frozen in Time

As my assignments at *GMA* spanned an ever-widening range of topics, venues, and purposes, the program's producers continually tried to dream up new themes and more creative situations for my on-the-road reports. One of the most brilliant ideas—yet, most uncomfortable for me—was "Spencer's Great North-to-South Adventure." Before I describe it, let me tell you how this idea was born.

Within my first two years on the show, it had become widely known to regular viewers (and *GMA* producers) that I had a low tolerance for cold weather. In fact, I hated it! Whenever I was on a location where the temperature was near or below freezing, you could see me shivering every time I appeared on camera. It actually became sort of a running joke. As Charlie and Joan would toss to me in a cold, snowy location, they would describe to me how warm and cozy they felt back in the studio. This generated lots of laughs and gained me tons of sympathy from viewers—many of whom sent me scarves, earmuffs, hats, gloves, and other items to keep me warm.

And so my great North-to-South adventure was born. It was a weeklong assignment in February 1996. The trip would begin at a very cold spot in the far north and take me to points farther south, and presumably warmer, each day. This was the itinerary:

Monday: Quebec City, Quebec
Tuesday: Killington, Vermont
Wednesday: Washington, D.C.
Thursday: Savannah, Georgia

Friday: Key West, Florida

I arrived in Quebec City on the Saturday before my broadcast week was to begin. The annual event known as Winter Carnival was underway, and the weather conditions certainly matched the theme. On each of the three days I was there, the wind-chill factor was minus 70, as in *70 degrees below zero!* Although I wasn't scheduled to be on the air until Monday, there was much setup work to be done over the weekend, and I had to be out in that brutally cold weather for several hours of prep work. It was the most painful chill I had ever felt. When I went to bed Sunday night, I felt anxious, almost frightened, about the next morning's broadcast.

My wake-up call came at 4:00 a.m. I got up and put on so many layers of clothing that I waddled rather than walked down the hall to the elevator. From the moment I stepped outside my hotel, I felt like a six-foot-two icicle. Within just a few minutes, a crust of ice had formed on my mustache. My facial muscles quickly became numb and tight, almost frozen. I couldn't enunciate clearly. I was on location from about 6:00 to 9:00 a.m., with no place to duck inside and get warm between my on-air segments. This was the worst discomfort I have felt in my entire life.

In nearly all of my eight or nine appearances on the air during those three hours, I was either interviewing or describing some hearty souls who were reveling in the deep chill of Carnaval de Québec. In one segment, I interviewed snow bathers who showed up in swimsuits and rolled around in the ice and snow. I winced and shivered as I watched them. Each time Charlie and Joan tossed to me, my speech sounded more slurred and mumbly as my facial muscles tightened in the freezing cold.

When 9:00 a.m. finally rolled around, I was taken back to my hotel, where I had to sit near a fireplace for about 45 minutes before I could function. I was thankful that day one of North-to-South had ended. But my cold-weather anxiety had not yet ended. The forecast for day two in Killington, Vermont, was for conditions almost identical to what I had just endured.

Surely enough, when I arrived in Killington that same afternoon, the wind chill was exactly minus 70 degrees. I was beginning to feel depressed, until I received some encouraging information about the format for day two. Although I would be broadcasting outside in frigid conditions at a ski resort, I would be able to relax and warm up at a nearby café during the breaks between my on-camera appearances. Day two of North-to-South was indeed crazy cold, but I was in much less pain and discomfort than I had been on day one.

As I was packing up to leave Killington, I couldn't wait to arrive in Washington, D.C., where it had to be warmer than my first two locations. Well, it was less cold, but that didn't quite qualify as warmer. On the evening before day three, the temperature in the nation's capital dropped into the single digits. Of course, I was at an outdoor location again for my broadcast, and when we went on the air at 7:00 a.m., the temperature was 12 degrees—but at least it was *above* zero! Day three turned out to be tolerable, certainly more comfortable than days one and two. And now I was looking forward to peeling off some layers of heavy clothing in sunny Savannah, Georgia.

When I arrived in Savannah on Wednesday afternoon, the weather wasn't quite what I had hoped for. The forecast for Thursday, day four of North-to-South, called for the coldest February day on record for Savannah. Just before broadcast time Thursday morning, the temperature reached a record low of 18 degrees. Once again, this was a treat compared to the 70-below wind chill I had encountered on days one and two, but when was it going to turn warm on this trip? How far south would I have to go?

The answer to that question might have been Aruba! When the day-four show ended in Savannah, I was off to my final North-to-South destination—Key West, Florida. It wasn't exactly balmy when I arrived, but the temperature was near 60 degrees and felt heavenly compared the deep freeze that had followed me southward the previous four days. Day five on Friday morning found me stationed at a historic saloon in Key West. The temperature at 7:00 a.m. was 56 degrees—cool by Florida Keys standards, but it brought a smile and a thaw to my face. And it brought an end to one of the cleverest ideas the *GMA* producers ever concocted for sending me on the road.

Making Richard Nixon Laugh

Among the notable people I've met and interviewed in my career are six US presidents: Richard Nixon, Gerald Ford, Jimmy Carter, George H. W. Bush, Barack Obama, and Donald Trump. And I'm proud to say that I hold the distinction of having made President Nixon laugh. Now, just in case this doesn't strike you as a noteworthy achievement, let me remind you that Nixon was not known for his sense of humor. In fact, he was generally known for his rather stern and serious demeanor.

Just a few months before his death, the former president appeared as a guest on *GMA*. Wanting to add another name to the list of presidents I had met, I decided to go to the green room prior to Nixon's scheduled segment and chat him up. I knew that he was an avid baseball fan, because he was often seen in the owner's box at New York Mets games at the old Shea Stadium, so I strode confidently into the green room, said, "Good Morning, Mr. President," and began talking with him about how the Mets were doing that season.

Within a few short minutes, we were having a lively and friendly conversation. As it became clear that he felt comfortable with me, I decided to tell him a true story that poked a little fun at him. I said, "Mr. President, in 1960, when you were running against John Kennedy, I was in the eighth grade. My civics teacher chose two students to do a mock presidential debate. I was Richard Nixon, and the other kid was John Kennedy. I won the debate—and you lost the election!" He let out a hearty laugh and said he was sorry to have let me down. I was relieved that he found my story amusing, and everyone who witnessed our conversation was shocked that I had the courage to tell him that story. Apparently, the casino was not the only place where I was willing to take risks.

Getting to Know Jimmy Carter

I have had the privilege and pleasure of interviewing former president Jimmy Carter three times. Yet, I have actually spent more time with him—quality time—away from the television cameras, observing the way he lives his life, and those "real life" moments were even more special than the interviews. But, long before I met the former president, I met his headline-making brother, Billy Carter, and had it not been for Billy, I might not have gotten to know Jimmy Carter so well.

In 1981, when I was hosting *Good Morning New York* for WABC-TV, Billy Carter was the subject of many news reports, because his rather "free-spirited" public behavior was such a sharp contrast to the more reserved demeanor of his brother, the president. So, my producers booked Billy and his wife, Sybil, as guests on our show. Much of the reporting on Billy's unorth-odox antics had portrayed him as a goofy hillbilly, which struck me as unfair. So, having no agenda other than letting Billy and Sybil reveal themselves to the viewing audience, I did what I considered to be a thoughtful, respectful interview with them. They were terrific guests—warm, engaging, and funny—and we exchanged hugs and handshakes at the end of the show.

Now, fast-forward to 1988. *GMA* was broadcasting from the site of the Democratic National Convention in Atlanta, and on the first day of our weeklong coverage, I reported from the Jimmy Carter Presidential Library and Museum with the former president as my first guest. At about 6:00 a.m., as my camera crew and I were getting set up on the property's magnif-icent lawn, we saw Jimmy Carter, an avid runner in those days, doing his morning run with a Secret Service agent. When he noticed us, he ran up to me, extended his hand, and said in his genteel Southern accent—as if he needed an introduction—"Hi, Spencer. I'm Jimmy Carter," and he expressed the Carter fami-ly's gratitude for the courtesy I had shown Billy and Sybil seven years earlier. I was stunned—also honored and gratified, but mostly stunned—that such a simple gesture of kindness from so many years before would be remembered and mentioned by a former president of the United States. It's also important to note that Billy was battling terminal cancer at that time, so those sentiments had even deeper meaning. Just over an hour later, the former president returned—dressed up for TV this time—and gave us a very thoughtful and interesting interview about the upcoming presidential election.

A few years later, around 1992, as Jimmy and Rosalynn Carter were becoming widely known for their work with Habi-tat for Humanity—building safe, affordable housing for people in need—*GMA* sent me to do a live remote at the site of one of their work projects in Washington, D.C. During the two-hour broadcast, I did several brief interviews with the Carters and was deeply impressed by how involved they were in doing the actual work of building that house. They surely were not seeking publicity. In fact, much to the contrary, Jimmy Carter seemed mildly annoyed that we kept interrupting his work and sticking a TV camera in his face, but he graciously tolerated our intrusions.

So, my "workday" with the Carters ended and I left with fond memories, not knowing whether I would ever see the former first couple again. But, in 1999, shortly after I relocated to ABC7/KGO-TV in San Francisco, a Carter family representative contacted me and asked if I would serve as emcee for Jimmy Carter's 75th birthday celebration in Americus, Georgia. I had to pinch myself. Was this for real? It was! So, in October 1999, I had the incredible honor of emceeing this grand event—and it was truly grand!

Carter's 75th birthday celebration was a formal affair, held at the historic Rylander Theatre. More than 600 people attended, including diplomats, foreign dignitaries, prominent political figures, entertainers, and journalists. Among the speakers paying tribute to the former president were White House correspondents Sam Donaldson of ABC News and Helen Thomas of United Press International, former US senator and disabled Vietnam War veteran Max Cleland, and singers Pat Boone and the McGuire Sisters. It was one of the most memorable events I've ever attended, and certainly the most memorable one I've ever emceed.

My last encounter with Jimmy Carter was in 2009. I interviewed him in San Francisco when he was on a promotional tour for his book *We Can Have Peace in the Holy Land*. He was 85 then, and just as sharply focused and engaging as ever. There are precious few people as deeply committed to promoting social justice and human dignity as Jimmy Carter. The humanitarian work he has done post-presidency is unsurpassed by any political figure, perhaps any public figure I can name. Of all the prominent people I've met who wear the label "Christian," no one is more Christ-like than Jimmy Carter.

Interviewing Barack Obama, Pre-Presidency

In late 2006, the political world was abuzz with speculation that US senator Barack Obama was going to announce his candidacy for the Democratic nomination for president. Just two years earlier, he had achieved the political equivalent of rock star status by giving a powerfully passionate and eloquent keynote speech at the Democratic National Convention. And now, in November 2006, Senator Obama was on a tour in San Francisco promoting his latest book, *The Audacity of Hope*, but the book tour was widely viewed as mainly a tune-up for the much-anticipated announcement of his presidential candidacy.

I was hosting a talk show called *The View from the Bay* at that time, and my co-host, Janelle Wang, and I had the honor of interviewing the young senator. When Senator Obama entered our studio, several staff members swooned over him. He was tall, handsome, charismatic, almost regal in his bearing, yet warm and approachable, with a smile that lit up the studio. He was also really smart! Of course, he was just a bit coy in fielding questions about when he might announce his candidacy. In fact, predictably, he did not even acknowledge that he planned to run. Yet, three months later, he made it official. And so, I had added another name to the list of presidents I had met and interviewed—and the first black president at that!

One of the most memorable moments in the interview was his response to a question that had nothing to do with politics—well, not really. In the book, then Senator Obama had referred to his younger self as "that skinny kid with the big ears." So, after a series of more serious questions, I asked, "When did that skinny kid with the big ears first think that he might like to be president of the United States someday?" His grin was wider than his face as he let out a hearty laugh, but he didn't give a direct answer, because that would have meant acknowledging that he intended to run. Sometimes, though, a facial expression says it all.

Dealing with Donald—Trump, That Is

Having interviewed and spent off-camera time with both Hillary Clinton and Donald Trump, I knew that the 2016 presidential election would yield me one more name to add to the list of presidents I'd met and interviewed. That list has now grown to six.

My interactions with Trump span a period of about ten years from the mid-1980s to mid-1990s, and a wide range of events and venues. I first interviewed him in 1985, when he owned the New Jersey Generals of the now defunct Unites States Football League, or the USFL. I was a sportscaster for WABC-TV at the time, and the future president was spearheading an effort to establish the USFL as a direct competitor with the storied National Football League, or NFL. This was during my high-roller days, and shortly after interviewing the brash billionaire I began frequenting his sparkling Atlantic City establishment, Trump Plaza Hotel and Casino.

My next interview with "The Donald," as his then wife, Ivana, called him, was done as we sat in a boxing ring at the Atlantic City Convention Center, the site of Mike Tyson's 1987 heavyweight title defense against Tyrell Biggs. The fight was hosted by Trump Plaza, and Donald showed up at 7:00 a.m. to talk with me on *GMA* about the big championship fight coming up that night. His public image was a bit softer in those days, and he had an undeniable star quality that made him a darling of the media. Shortly after that interview and the exposure he received on *GMA*, I found myself on the invitation list to all of Donald Trump's exclusive VIP parties at Trump Plaza and later at the Trump Taj Mahal hotel and casino, which opened in 1990.

His VIP parties were legendary. Invited guests usually included Oprah, Muhammad Ali, Howard Stern, and countless luminaries from the worlds of sports, entertainment, and media, as well as a select group of high rollers who frequented his casinos. I fell into two of those categories.

Talking with Trump in this setting was far different from interviewing him on camera, as his language was a bit more colorful and unfiltered. I can't offer any quotes here, because I want this book to pass legal review and get published. Suffice it to say that certain events during the 2016 presidential campaign provided a taste of the Trumpspeak that I encountered at his private events, but that I would not have been able to air on *GMA*.

In 1993, Donald Trump attempted to launch a cable network talk show featuring his then wife Marla Maples, and he wanted me to be her co-host. My bosses at *GMA* gave me permission to explore the opportunity, and I attended a big planning meeting with Donald, Marla, and a couple of veteran talk-show producers, but the program never got off the ground.

What was perhaps my most unusual interaction with Trump occurred in the mid-1990s, during one of the deepest downward spirals of my gambling "career." I had suffered a series of severe losses, and my financial house of cards was on the verge of collapse. Having run out of conventional lending institutions to borrow from, I was feeling weak-kneed and desperate. So, I decided to turn to my pal, Donald, for a loan. I composed a carefully crafted letter describing my short-term need and, swallowing every ounce of pride and self-respect, faxed the letter to him in his executive office at Trump Tower. I had gained access to his direct phone lines during an exclusive, off-camera interview. The day after I faxed my loan proposal, he called me at my home number. He said he was sorry for what I was going through, but he couldn't lend me money because he was being audited and his financial transactions were under intense scrutiny.

In light of the paths we have both traveled since then, I am thankful that president-to-be Donald Trump did not become my creditor.

Jerry Ford Was a Fan of Mine

Gerald Ford was a guest on *GMA* in 1994. This was shortly after the death of Richard Nixon, the man Ford had succeeded as president, and whom he later pardoned for his role in the Watergate scandal. Charlie Gibson was scheduled to do the interview. And, since I was not going to be involved in the segment, I decided to drop by the green room and introduce myself, thereby adding another name to the growing list of presidents I had met. The moment I stepped into the green room, the former president popped up from his seat and exclaimed, "Spencer! Betty and I watch you every morning!" I felt so honored. He gave me a vigorous handshake and said how pleased he was to meet me. I expressed the same sentiment to him and told him I was amazed that someone as busy as a president, even a former president, would pay much attention to "a mere weatherman," but he assured me that I was one of his and Betty's favorite television personalities.

It's fun being me!

Chapter Six

As the year 1999 began, I was facing the most challenging and depressing time of my life. My final contract at *GMA* had expired, and I was moving to San Francisco to work for the ABC-owned station there. This was a wonderful opportunity, for which I was grateful, but it meant leaving the national spotlight of network TV for the much more limited exposure of local news. It also meant a nearly 50 percent reduction in salary. At the same time, Diane had decided to leave me. So, after 29 years of marriage, I was going through a divorce—a very painful and expensive divorce. I was devastated.

Now, let me be clear about the changes and challenges facing me at this time. I had enjoyed a series of lucrative contracts at *GMA* in my nearly thirteen-year run. One of the realities of the television industry is that the passage of time brings change. Viewers' tastes and tendencies change, and audience demographics change as well. In order to accommodate those changes and remain relevant and competitive, familiar faces on programs like *GMA* and *Today* change from time to time. As I entered the final year of my last *GMA* contract, my longtime co-hosts, Charlie and Joan, had already departed the show—although Charlie did return for the rebuilding of *GMA* a year later. I truly have no reason to believe that my gambling was a significant factor in the non-renewal of my last contract. The program was simply going through a changing of the guard. My high-roller lifestyle was certainly well known at ABC, but there was never an indication that management had a problem with it. In fact, *GMA* had sent me on countless assignments to Las Vegas and Atlantic City, covering various sports and entertainment events. So, if ABC executives viewed my gambling as an issue, they certainly showed no signs of concern. I was not eager to leave *GMA*, but to this day I feel nothing but gratitude for the way I was treated by the ABC brass.

Getting back to the issue of Diane's demand for a divorce, the logical question for someone looking from the outside is, "Was your gambling a factor?" I would be foolish to claim that it was not a factor, but I take Diane's word that it was not at the top of her list of reasons. Diane is a fine and honorable woman with many wonderful qualities. We were life partners for nearly 30 years and raised two amazing children together. I have too much respect for Diane's privacy to divulge her personal and heartfelt reasons for wanting a divorce, but I will share this: in our many tear-filled, heart-to-heart conversations, my gambling was always mentioned as a secondary reason. Diane is honest and straightforward; she does not pull punches. She wanted a new and independent life, and I take her at her word.

But that didn't make starting a new life any less painful for me. I can look back now at my dramatic life changes in 1999 with some measure of clarity and composure. At that time, however, I felt like the world I had known and loved was ending. How had this happened so suddenly? My companion of three decades, the mother of my children, wanted a new life on her own. The job I had cherished was now just another entry on my résumé. I was relocating 3,000 miles away from everything and everyone dear to me. And my financial pressures were growing exponentially. Divorce settlement, severe cut in pay, outstanding balances on casino credit lines, and mounting tax debt—I was living in a constant state of worry. It was difficult to sleep at night and hard to smile during the day. I worried constantly about money problems and how to meet my obligations. But I was much more torn apart by the loss of my marriage and family life. My sadness and anxiety actually caused me to have physical pain—headaches, lower-back pain, tightness of the muscles in my neck and shoulders. I couldn't relax when I got in bed at night. It sometimes took hours to fall asleep.

And the emotional pain was even greater. I cried every day for months after moving to San Francisco. I would sometimes cry while standing in the shower, and let the water wash away my tears. I began psychological counseling and poured out my problems in therapy. Going to the gym every day was also helpful, but mainly during the hour or so that I was working out. As soon as I was showered and dressed, the sadness would set in again. Prayer was valuable, as it always had been, but I had to continually remind myself that my present condition was many years in the making, so I perhaps shouldn't expect God to provide me with sudden and miraculous healing. Nonetheless, I couldn't escape my feelings of sadness, confusion, worry, and depression. I felt lost and overwhelmed, and I was unable to hide it.

During the first six months in my new job at KGO-TV, I was like a zombie—a mere shell of my usual self—and it showed on the air. Many viewers who had followed me on *GMA* wrote to ask if I was okay. They could tell that something was missing.

The quick wit and positive energy that had defined my personality on *GMA* were visibly dimmed, sometimes completely absent from my on-air presentation. It was comforting that viewers cared enough to write and ask how I was adjusting, but it also made me wonder if I would ever climb out of that sinking pit. I was a bit trance-like walking around the station, too. I would speak to people I encountered in the hallways, but sometimes seconds later I had forgotten the person to whom I had just spoken. I was an emotional mess.

As I had done in virtually every difficult circumstance in my life, I turned to God for guidance and answers. Now, let me be very clear about this. I am not someone who goes crying to God only in hard times. I have sought and felt God's presence in all circumstances. But at that time, with what felt like an unbearable burden, I sought an even deeper spiritual connection. I hoped for a miracle but prayed for comfort, strength, guidance, and wisdom. I adopted a local church as my regular place of worship. I joined a Bible study group. I spent more time in prayer and quiet reflection. *But*—I also continued my foolish effort to keep juggling those casino credit lines. When I wasn't flying out to Las Vegas on a Sunday after church to pay off and renew those markers, I was making weekend flights to Atlantic City to do the same thing there. To say that this routine was exhausting is a huge understatement.

Near the end of 1999, I approached my breaking point. I had undoubtedly experienced a good measure of spiritual growth and felt much more comfortable with my new life in California, but the weight of my financial worries was crushing. My casino debt was undiminished, and the Internal Revenue Service was after me again. I had fallen two years behind on federal income taxes, and the IRS was threatening to come after me with the heavy artillery—liens and wage attachment. This situation called for some serious self-examination. As a person of faith, I asked God for help, but at the same time I let my pride get in the way. I was trying to avoid the uncomfortable but necessary step of telling the casinos that I had maxed out and simply could not afford to pay them off all at once. I would have to negotiate some kind of payoff plan. I should have done this a year earlier, but I lacked the moral courage. Now I had arrived at a critical moment of reckoning. What should my next step be?

The answer came within a matter of days. It came shockingly, frighteningly—and miraculously.

✳   ✳   ✳

I was awakened on a Monday morning by a phone call around 8:00 a.m. The caller identified himself as an FBI agent from the New York district office, and he informed me that I had been under criminal investigation for one year—an investigation that he had just concluded. The bottom fell out of my stomach, and my heart began pounding. My left hand trembled as it held the phone. Then, just as I was about to collapse in a state of complete panic, the agent told me that no charge was being brought against me. His investigation had led him to the conclusion that I had not committed any criminal offense. He added, however, that I clearly had a gambling problem and that the manner in which I had been moving money around was what had led to my being investigated.

Here's what I had been doing that drew the FBI's attention and triggered the investigation. Before every casino credit line "juggling" trip, I would withdraw several thousand dollars from each of the numerous checking accounts that I maintained. Then, upon returning home, I would redeposit into my various accounts whatever cash I had brought back. Because cash deposits and withdrawals of $10,000 or more require a bit of paperwork (it's federal banking law), I kept all of my individual transactions under $10,000 in order to save time and avoid the paperwork hassle. However, since I had maintained this pattern for so long—depositing $7,500 here and $8,000 there—my banks became suspicious and reported the pattern of my transactions to the federal government. The FBI then began investigating my activities to see if I was engaged in any illegal activity or was perhaps committing some form of bank fraud. Thankfully, I was deemed not to have broken the law, but the investigating agent filled me in on all that he had learned about me.

He had interviewed employees at the banks where I maintained accounts, casino personnel who knew me from my regular visits, and many other people I encountered in my travels and financial transactions. He had even spoken with colleagues of mine at *GMA* who were familiar with my frequent trips to gambling venues. His final words to me were an admonition. He strongly suggested that I get some professional help to deal with my gambling addiction—and then told me that my case was closed. This had truly been a wake-up call, literally and figuratively.

As I recovered from the shock of that call, I quietly gave thanks. In my mind, this had been the answer to many prayers—the jolt or reality check that I needed. The next step I had been looking for was now right in front of me. I needed to stop the charade. I called all the casinos where I had credit lines—14 of them—and pleaded my case. I described my weakened financial condition and inability to settle all of my obligations at once, and asked for reasonable payoff plans. Interestingly enough, the

ones to whom I owed the highest amounts—$40,000 or more—
were the most cooperative and offered me the most affordable
payment plans. The ones to whom I owed the lowest amounts—
under $20,000—were completely uncooperative and employed
aggressive collection tactics, filing judgments against me and
serving me with papers at work, in full view of my colleagues.

Confronting the casinos and dealing with the fallout was
difficult and humiliating, but it was also liberating. I no longer
had to play the risky and exhausting juggling act that I had
carried on for years, and I could reclaim some semblance of a
normal life. Just before New Year's Day in 2000, I made what
I thought would be my last visit to Las Vegas or any other
gambling venue.

✳ ✳ ✳

I felt stronger and happier during the first few months of the
new millennium than I had felt in a very long time. I still had
to deal with huge financial obligations—alimony, back taxes,
casino payoffs—but my life felt manageable again. And, by
now I was beginning to hit my stride at work. Zombie Spencer
had faded away, and my natural joie de vivre was much more
evident. Nonetheless, my money problems were real, and
they were considerable. The IRS was pressuring me for bigger
payments on my back taxes, the casinos were also demanding
faster repayment, alimony wouldn't end for another six years,
and my new income was never going to rise anywhere near the
level of my old *GMA* paychecks. So, even with my new lease on
life, financial pressures persisted.

I called my longtime attorney and dear friend, Irv Brodsky,
who had been with me through thick and thin. Irv had repre-
sented me during my first bout with the IRS, mediated my

divorce settlement with Diane, and even lent me money during some of my most trying times. Surely, Irv would offer me wise counsel. Well, after many hours of budget analysis and settlement talks with the IRS, Irv concluded that I would have to file bankruptcy—again. It would not eliminate my tax liability, alimony payments, or any secured obligations, but it would wipe out the gambling debt, and that would relieve a tremendous amount of financial pressure.

So, in 2001, for the second time in seventeen years, I filed Chapter 7 bankruptcy. My self-esteem sank. I was repeating a very sad and shameful bit of my personal history. In the broader view of my life, I felt like a good and decent person. But now that I was going through bankruptcy number two, "good" and "decent" were not the first two words I would use to describe myself—and certainly not "smart." As the date approached for my preliminary hearing before the trustee of the bankruptcy court, I became increasingly nervous. And when that day finally arrived, my worst fears were realized.

There were about 200 people in the courtroom, and I was one of dozens of bankruptcy petitioners who would be called out in front of the assembled crowd to answer questions from the trustee. Many in the room recognized me before my name was called. I couldn't wait for this nightmare to end, but I knew that I had brought it on myself. Finally, the trustee called out, "Edward Spencer Christian, Jr." I stood up and acknowledged that was my full name. He then proceeded to interrogate me for about 15 minutes about my numerous debts and creditors.

"Do you owe Casino X $50,000?"

"Yes."

"Do you owe Casino Y $40,000?"

"Yes."

"Did you at one time work for ABC News and *Good Morning America*?"

"Yes."

"And was your annual salary at one time over $1 million?"

"Yes."

"And you are now seeking bankruptcy relief?"

"Yes."

It felt like the longest 15 minutes of my life—and perhaps it should have. Every eye in the room was focused on me. I had never felt more ashamed of myself. At that moment, I did not have one shred of self-respect. I could only imagine how some of the others in that room must have felt as they listened to my case. Nearly all of the other petitioners appeared to be low-wage earners who had probably never dreamed of earning the kind of money I had foolishly thrown away. I kept reminding myself that I deserved this humiliation—I had earned it!

Within a matter of days, the supermarket tabloids had published stories about my bankruptcy accompanied by pictures of me getting out of my car, walking into the grocery store, leaving the gym, and entering a bank. I had been followed! The tabloid reporters were almost as good at investigating as the FBI had been. Their stories were relatively accurate, with only minor exaggerations, and they contained quotes about my gambling and finances that could only have come from people who actually knew me personally.

I suddenly began getting requests for interviews from mainstream news outlets. Each time, I simply acknowledged that I'd had a long-term gambling problem and that I was indeed going through a bankruptcy, and stated that I had quit gambling at least a year prior to the bankruptcy. After about a month of tabloid exposure, the story quietly went away. However, there was one awkward moment that I found both embarrassing and amusing. At the height of my tabloid celebrity, I was standing in the checkout line at my local grocery store, and the woman directly in front of me was reading about me without realizing that I was standing right behind her. When I noticed what she was reading, I quickly turned my cart around and headed for another checkout line several aisles away.

One of the most remarkable things about this bankruptcy experience was that ABC did not discard me. Much to the contrary, when I approached the president and general manager of the station prior to my filing Chapter 7 and laid all of my cards on the table, so to speak, he was sympathetic, compassionate, and supportive. He asked only that I not allow my personal challenges to affect the quality of my work, and that I seek professional help if I felt myself slipping back into the grips of gambling. I could not have asked more from an employer than that. I will be forever grateful to ABC for its solid support.

In early 2002, my case was closed. I was left with alimony payments, tax debt, and other obligations that were not erased in bankruptcy, but the casino debts were discharged and I was given yet another fresh start, a chance to turn my life around. This was what I had hoped for, what I had prayed for. I was running out of second chances, but as low as I had sunk this time around, I hadn't hit rock bottom yet. I was due for one more dance with the devil.

The Christian family, 1954: Spencer, Sr.; Lucy; my younger brother Lutrell (age three); and me (age seven), at the home of one of my uncles in Charles City, Virginia. (Inset) Sixth-grade photo at Ruthville School in Charles City, Virginia; age 11.

(Top) *With my mom on the front lawn of our home in Charles City, Virginia; summer 1960, just before my 13th birthday.*

(Bottom) *Graduation photo from Ruthville High School, Charles City, Virginia; 1965, age 17.*

PHOTO © American Broadcasting Companies, Inc.

(Top left) *Sophomore year at Hampton Institute (now Hampton University), in Hampton, Virginia; age 19.*

(Top right) *Senior year at Hampton Institute; age 21.*

(Bottom) *In the studio at WABC-TV in New York City, summer of 1977. I was 29 and had just moved to New York a few months earlier, in the sixth year of my career.*

My then-wife Diane and I chat with Muhammad Ali at a VIP party at Trump Plaza Hotel-Casino in Atlantic City, New Jersey, in 1988.

PHOTO © American Broadcasting Companies, Inc.

On the GMA set in early 1989, before Joan lost the "big hair."

Filling in for Charlie Gibson as co-host in 1989. I often filled in for Joan Lunden, as well. My co-hosting with Charlie gave morning TV a new look—two male hosts—but, apparently, our viewers didn't suffer from testosterone turnoff, as ratings remained strong.

Weather duet with Bill Murray in the early 1990s. This was at least a year before he played a TV weatherman in the movie Groundhog Day.

PHOTO © American Broadcasting Companies, Inc.

PHOTO © American Broadcasting Companies, Inc.

(Right) *Posing with Joan and Charlie in 1992, near the very peak of our popularity.*

(Bottom) *On "The Strip" in Las Vegas during a* GMA *road trip in 1994.*

PHOTO © American Broadcasting Companies, Inc.

PHOTO © American Broadcasting Companies, Inc.

(Top) *With baseball Hall-of-Famer Duke Snider at the GMA studio in the early 1990s.*

(Left) *Dionne Warwick on my farewell broadcast at GMA on December 22, 1998. The second hour of the program was a tribute to me. Tom Hanks sent a video-taped message. Muhammad Ali sent an autographed portrait. George Steinbrenner called to wish me well. And Dionne Warwick sang "Do You Know the Way to San Francisco," a variation on her hit song "Do You Know the Way to San Jose."*

With President and Mrs. Carter at the former president's 75th birthday celebration in 1999.

With Oprah in Chicago, September 2009. ABC7/KGO-TV sent me to interview Oprah following the announcement that 2009–2010 would be the last season of her show.

PHOTO © American Broadcasting Companies, Inc.

"Throwback Thursday" on GMA in 2014. I was filling in for Ginger Zee as she prepared for her wedding and honeymoon. It was my first time in the GMA studio since 2005, and I had a blast—it felt like I'd never left!

Chapter Seven

As 2002 rolled around, it had been two years since I had last entered a casino. I was still paying off a hefty IRS debt, sizable monthly alimony, and other heavy financial burdens, but I felt a level of peace and freedom I hadn't enjoyed in many years. Those days of desperation—hoping to hit a winning streak, losing sleep over money matters—seemed like something from the distant past.

By this time, I had also met Lyn, the woman who would later become my second wife. Nearly every weekend, we ventured off to some California wine country destination, indulging our passion for wine and food. Interestingly enough, although Lyn had Italian ancestors, she had not been introduced to wine before she met me. I, on the other hand, had been a passionate wine enthusiast for decades. I had even hosted a TV wine show for many years. And now, Lyn was not only my companion but also my "wine protégée."

Doing the wine show was just about the most fun I could imagine having and getting paid for, and it seemed to drop into my lap out of nowhere. I had been a serious wine lover and collector for about ten years before I joined *GMA*, and I took every opportunity to talk about my passion for wine on the air—especially during cooking segments with fabulous chefs like Julia Child, Jacques Pépin, Wolfgang Puck, and Emeril Lagasse. So, it was widely known that I fancied myself a connoisseur. One morning in early 1994, right after I got off the air at *GMA*, I received a call from an old friend and former ABC colleague who now headed a company that was producing programs for a new cable network called Home and Garden Television, or HGTV. He asked if I was interested in hosting a show about wine. The HGTV executives were looking for someone with vast wine knowledge who was also well known to the public. I couldn't say yes fast enough, and the result was *Spencer Christian's Wine Cellar*, a weekly half-hour show that enjoyed a five-year run from January 1995 to January 2000. Of course, I needed the approval of my bosses at ABC, and I was thrilled to get their okay.

The show covered virtually every aspect of wine appreciation: different grape varieties and how they are grown, the winemaking process from the vine to the bottle, food and wine pairing, proper storage of wine, the best wine bargains, wine etiquette—how to swirl, sniff, and sip—and much more. I did segments in vineyards with winemakers, in kitchens with famous chefs, in stores with wine merchants, and in my own personal cellar. The show was a hit. It was one of the most popular shows on HGTV during that network's first three years on the air, and it added another dimension to my public persona.

Shooting segments for my show also enabled me to further indulge my gambling addiction, as many of our shoots occurred in the wine country of California or in the kitchens and wine cellars of celebrity chefs at their new restaurants in Las Vegas, which enjoyed a culinary explosion in the 1990s. I would often leave the *GMA* studio after a Friday-morning broadcast and dash off to catch a flight to one of those western destinations. At the end of a shoot late Friday night or early Saturday morning, I would spend the remainder of the weekend in the Vegas casinos before returning home late Sunday evening, just in time to get a few hours' sleep before my 3:30 a.m. wake-up call for *GMA* on Monday. I honestly don't know how I survived such a hectic pace. I generally didn't get more than about two hours of sleep during those overnight stops in Las Vegas. I do know that I was driven by the joy I derived from work and my compulsive urge to gamble.

* * *

Returning to the story of my fourth year in San Francisco—my third year of being "clean"—the events of 2002 continued to point to a new, healthier, happier life for me. In June, I received a call from my dear friend and former *Good Morning America* colleague Julia Child, the legendary TV chef. Julia's 90th birthday was coming up, and she asked me to emcee her big celebration. I was so excited! Even though I had known Julia for 25 years, I still felt incredibly honored that she wanted me as her emcee.

What an amazing extravaganza this turned out to be—a two-day celebration held in downtown Napa at Copia, the American Center for Wine, Food & the Arts. Day one was the actual birthday dinner, attended by Robert and Margrit Mondavi, Jacques Pépin, a production crew from ABC-TV's *Nightline*, and more than a hundred of the most prominent people in the arena of food and wine. On day two, Julia held a press conference in Copia's cooking demonstration room, which was laid out more like an auditorium. Nearly a hundred media members showed up from all over the world, and Julia insisted that I sit on her right while her sister, Dorothy, sat on her left to help field the questions.

It was during this press conference that Julia said perhaps the funniest words I'd ever heard come out of her mouth, and I'd heard her say some hilarious things. Following numerous questions about her life, career, and favorite recipes, someone asked her this: "If you had only one meal left to eat in your life, what would it be?" And Julia replied, "A hamburger and a glass of whiskey!" Waves of riotous laughter filled the room for about two or three minutes. Who would have expected this world-famous chef to find pleasure in such a simple meal?

$$* \quad * \quad *$$

The year 2002 continued to be a promising year of "recovery" for me, until a challenging invitation came along. In October, I heard from a longtime friend who was a casino executive in Las Vegas. He was planning his 50th birthday party, and he invited me not only to attend but also to be a participant. Rick's birthday dinner was going to be a roast. He had invited a couple of dozen sports and entertainment celebrities to be guest roasters, and he wanted me to be among them.

It's hard to describe how I felt about this invitation. I wanted to be there for my friend's 50th birthday and was excited about the prospect of being one of his celebrity roasters. There was also a part of me that wanted to prove I could go to Las Vegas for an event like this and resist the urge to gamble. I truly did not feel a conscious urge. But the people closest to me, Lyn and my kids, were concerned. They were intimately acquainted with the misery I had brought on myself through gambling, and they thought it was unwise for me to be in the casino environment.

I certainly understood their concern, but the more I thought about it, the more I wanted to prove something—that I could go to Vegas just for this special event and not have a gambling relapse. So, Lyn and I were off to the desert.

The roast was a hit—and I was a hit. The star-studded lineup of roasters was led by legendary comic Alan King, yet my one-liners got the biggest laughs and several of the "pros" complimented me on how clever I was. My return to Vegas was off to a successful start. But perhaps I was feeling a bit too self-congratulatory.

After the party, Lyn was saddened, but not surprised, when I told her I was going down to the casino to "test myself." After a nearly three-year absence, I re-entered the danger zone. On the surface, the whole experience seemed rather benign. I spent just over an hour playing low-stakes craps and blackjack, lost a few hundred dollars, and then called it a night. But as I returned to my room, I knew that I would go back to the casino the next morning and try to recoup my losses. Surely enough, that's exactly what I did. Down to the casino I went around 6:30 a.m., as Lyn was packing for our return flight. I almost immediately caught a little winning streak, and then quickly cashed in my chips and raced up to our room, having won back the previous night's losses.

On the flight back to San Francisco, I tried to convince myself that this trip had been a victory for me, because I had not suffered a net loss and had spent only a limited amount of time in the casino. It was a pathetic attempt at self-deception. I had gone almost three years without gambling—without even thinking about returning to gambling—but this trip had left me with an unsettled, uncertain feeling about the road ahead.

Chapter Eight

Within a few months, by spring of 2003, I was frequenting Las Vegas again—nearly every other weekend—and enjoying the high-roller lifestyle. Lyn accompanied me on most of these trips, and she slowly seemed to embrace the fun and excitement. We stayed in VIP suites, dined at the finest restaurants, had front-row seats at the top shows, and everything was complimentary. A couple of things were different from the old days, though. I no longer qualified for credit lines because of my recent bankruptcy, and I limited my "action" to only one casino, Mandalay Bay. I chose that hotel because it was relatively new, exclusive, and upscale—and I had no history there.

I was actually ashamed to be seen at my old haunts. All of the dealers, credit managers, and other casino personnel who knew me from the old days would surely ask questions about my long absence, or about rumors they had heard concerning my "troubles," so I simply stayed away from those places. I spared myself some embarrassment and avoided painful reminders of the bad times.

Meanwhile, I was perfectly comfortable at Mandalay Bay. Having no access to casino credit, I took enough cash with me on each trip to play at a betting level that would easily qualify me for the comps I received. Every player in a casino is watched carefully by pit bosses and other employees, who keep close tabs on things such as initial buy-in amount, average bet size, amount of time "in action," and approximate amounts won or lost. This is how casinos rate players and determine the level of free stuff to extend. With that in mind, I began each session of play with a buy-in of about $5,000 and averaged about six hours of playing time per day—longer when Lyn wasn't with me. This earned me a high enough rating to qualify for the VIP treatment I received.

I reveled in a stunning winning streak at Mandalay Bay for a period of about six months. After nearly every session of play, I walked away with about $2,000 to $4,000 of profit. I would then place the winnings in my safe deposit box and take a break. That might mean going to the gym, hanging out with Lyn, or just taking a nap. After a relaxing break, I would return to the casino for more action. It was a routine that seemed to work. And, at the end of each trip, my safe deposit box contained about $10,000 to $15,000. I hadn't enjoyed a winning streak like that in 10 years, since the mid-1990s. I stored envelopes stuffed with $100 bills in my freezer at home, which I referred to as "cold cash." I was riding high again.

But I, more than anyone, knew that streaks don't last. It was only a matter of time. And sure enough, one Sunday evening the good times came to a screeching halt.

❋   ❋   ❋

After a weekend of fine dining, dazzling shows, and winning in the Mandalay Bay casino, I went to the VIP lounge to check out. But instead of being asked to sign the usual ALL EXPENSES

PAID form, I was handed a bill for $3,600. When I asked why I had to pay these charges, the lounge manager said I needed to contact my casino host, the person who arranged my accommodations and authorized my comps. In a hurry to catch my flight home, I paid the $3,600 with a credit card and called my host while en route to the airport. I got his voicemail, so I left a message explaining what had happened in the checkout lounge. When he didn't return my call that night, I began to get an uneasy feeling. I called and left messages for him four times over the next several days. He never called back. Then I knew what was up. Because of my long winning streak, I was no longer welcome.

Casino executives can be as strange and superstitious as gamblers. I have seen many cases of high rollers receiving the red-carpet treatment as long as their winnings were offset by losses. But when a player wins big on six or seven consecutive trips, some casino managers will tell the host to cut that player off, fearing that the casino is "unlucky" when that player shows up. It seems absurd to me or to anyone who understands the built-in advantage that casinos have over gamblers. Every single game in a casino has carefully calculated or "fixed" mathematical odds against the player. A gambler who has a lucky winning streak cannot hurt a casino's profitability. Yet, for as long as casinos have existed, players who have experienced long winning streaks have found themselves suddenly unwelcome where they had previously been treated like royalty.

What made my situation seem especially absurd is that I was at the low end of the so-called high rollers. My winning streak could not possibly have put a dent in the casino's profits. On the other hand, a really big-time high roller—known in gambling circles as a "whale"—could give a host or credit manager reason to be nervous. Whales usually put a couple of million dollars in play per day. When they have winning streaks, they can beat the casino for tens of millions. In gambling parlance, my winning streak at Mandalay Bay was chump change. Yet, it was big enough for someone there to force me to look for another place to play.

Following my banishment from Mandalay Bay, I began falling into another downward spiral. As I ventured into other Las Vegas casinos, my "cold cash" quickly melted away. I lost money on 11 consecutive trips. Changing venues didn't help—each casino I visited seemed unluckier than the one before. The year 2003 had begun on a sunny note but was turning terribly gloomy now. What could I do to turn things around?

One day, as I was losing bet after bet at a craps table, a sympathetic dealer suggested that I give poker a try. The game had become wildly popular in 2003 because of television coverage of the World Series of Poker, which is held each year in Las Vegas. The WSOP, as it is widely known, had previously generally attracted only professional poker players. But in 2003, an amateur player with the unlikely name of Chris Moneymaker won the top prize and became an instant millionaire. Almost overnight, "World Series" came to mean something other than baseball, and millions of people who had never gambled before were flooding casinos across the country to try their hand at poker. I hadn't played poker in many years, but I decided to give it a try.

By the middle of 2004, I had become strictly a poker player. No more craps, no more blackjack, and no more of the trappings of the high-roller lifestyle. Casinos don't offer comps to poker players, because they don't play against the house—they compete against other players. Casinos profit from poker by taking what is known as a "rake," a small fraction of the pot in each hand that is dealt, but there are no house-imposed odds. There are, however, mathematical odds of winning or losing any given hand based on a range of factors, including the tendencies and personality quirks that a player might observe in his or her opponents. The bottom line is that poker is largely a game of skill, although an element of chance certainly exists. So, being competitive by nature, I decided that poker was the game for me.

I soon found that I didn't miss the luxury suites or the gourmet meals, because I began winning regularly enough at poker to cover my travel expenses and modest accommodations. The vast majority of players who filled poker rooms during the game's explosion of popularity from 2003 to 2006 were easy prey for the more skillful and experienced players. Even I was a consistent winner during those first few years, primarily because of the vast number of unskilled, undisciplined players drawn to poker rooms by the lure of poker on TV and the dream of raking in massive piles of chips after winning a big hand. But poker as depicted on TV is a glamorized version of what is, in real life, often a very unglamorous grind. Nonetheless, I was thriving.

By 2009, about six years after poker had become a hit on TV, the weaker, less skillful players were going broke, poker rooms were becoming less crowded, and it was getting tougher and tougher for a player of my limited ability to win. But by the time I made this honest admission, I had begun playing in relatively high-stakes games. My occasional wins were comforting, but my frequent losses were demoralizing. Faster than I realized what was happening, I found myself slipping deeply into debt again. Typically, casino poker rooms don't offer credit lines. But there are so-called cardrooms in California that feature poker along with various other card games, and I found one in the Los Angeles area where I could open a small line of credit. It was Commerce Casino in the East Los Angeles city of Commerce. It's the world's largest poker room, and arguably most popular.

Now in full gambling relapse mode, I began bouncing between Commerce and the poker rooms in Las Vegas. Of the several variations of poker, my game of choice was No-Limit Hold 'Em, which allows you to risk the total amount of money or chips in front of you on a single bet—thrilling when you win, crushing when you lose! When I was losing on a Saturday night in Vegas, I would often rent a car, make the four-hour drive to Commerce, and spend Sunday trying to recoup my losses there.

There's an old gambling term called "chasing your losses." That's essentially what I was doing for the two-year period from 2009 to 2011, and it was wearing me down physically, financially, and spiritually. The frequent trips to Commerce and Las Vegas produced enough winning sessions to feed the fantasy of recovering my losses, but chasing losses often meant sitting at a poker table for more than 12 hours a day. In fact, I pulled more all-nighters playing poker as I entered my mid-60s than I did as a college student in the 1960s. It was an exhausting ordeal, but I couldn't see a way out—or maybe I just refused to.

In the spring of 2011, one particularly depressing weekend at Commerce forced me to do some serious soul-searching. I had spent nearly 20 hours in the poker room that weekend, unsuccessfully chasing losses. Now, during the six-hour drive home to San Francisco, I had a sudden awareness of my mortality. I was approaching my 64th birthday, and I wondered, "If I were to die today, what purpose would my life have served? And how would I be remembered, especially by my kids, whom

I love more than life itself?" As I wrestled with these questions, the overriding feeling was not fear but extreme sadness and disappointment. In the autumn of my life, and likely the closing years of my career, I was broke—absolutely flat broke and in deep debt because I was addicted to gambling. What was I prepared to do about it?

Chapter Nine

Of course, the first thing I needed to do was quit playing poker, and quit gambling altogether. That was something my rational mind had known for years. But did I have a true desire to quit, deep down inside? You see, gambling was not only an addiction but also a distraction. When I was playing poker, my mind was focused only on the game at hand. I wasn't thinking about real-life problems like how to deal with debt, even though poker was the source of that debt. Playing poker carried me off to a fantasyland where sleep wasn't important and where I might win enough money to pay back the friends from whom I had borrowed. Just two or three winning trips would enable me to pay off my credit-card balances. Then I could take a break from poker and get caught up on sleep, because the stress from losing would no longer keep me awake at night. Just one winning streak would make it easier for me to quit.

This is the twisted logic of the addict's mind. Your rational self may know the right thing to do, but the addicted self can easily convince you to make wrong choices. I felt certain that I wanted to quit, but I wanted to quit on my terms. I wanted to keep playing long enough to catch a little winning streak, pay off some debt, ease the financial pressure, and then walk away from gambling with my head held high. Right! What I really wanted was a fast and easy way out of my misery, but there was no such path.

A few years earlier, I had tried Gamblers Anonymous. I attended meetings once a week for six weeks. During that time, I did not play poker, but I concluded that GA was not the remedy for me. I felt that I needed a path with clearer markers along the way to help me measure my progress. Aha! Why not write a book about my struggles? For many years I had thought about writing an autobiography. Sharing my journey through the darkness of addiction would probably be cathartic, and it could offer hope and encouragement to others. Plus, the writing process might provide those progress markers I needed. So, I started calling close friends and family, telling them I was going to write a book revealing my addiction and describing how I "conquered" it.

I reached out to an old friend and former *Good Morning America* executive producer, George Merlis, for advice and guidance in my book venture. I trusted George's judgment and valued his publishing contacts. Over the next couple of months, we developed an outline for the book and a plan for pitching it to publishers. I was buzzing with excitement over my new endeavor and my determination to keep gambling in my past.

After completing a few sample chapters, I wanted to believe I had found a quick fix. Book sales and speaking engagements would help me recover my financial footing, and I would be done with gambling forever. But an email exchange with my dear friend Charlie Gibson gave me a sharp reality check. Charlie cautioned me to be absolutely sure I was on the road to recovery before making any public pronouncements. He reminded me of the tragic story of former NFL and Ohio State quarterback Art Schlichter, whose compulsive gambling ended his career, wrecked his marriage, and sent him to prison multiple times. His story was tragic. His legal problems included theft, fraud, forgery, passing bad checks, and involvement in illegal gambling operations. Between 1995 and 2006, he spent roughly ten years in prisons and jails across the Midwest. Schlichter had more than one relapse after claiming that he'd given up gambling. Charlie genuinely cared about my well-being and didn't want me to go public prematurely. My old buddy knew me well, and he saw the potential danger in my eagerness to proclaim freedom from the grip of gambling.

Not long after receiving Charlie's cautionary advice, I felt my resolve weakening. Gamblers like quick results, and this writing and publishing process was moving too slowly for me. I was restless and anxious—the classic characteristics of a compulsive gambler. Late one Wednesday night, in the middle of my workweek, I felt a sudden impulse—I wanted to play poker. I drove to a cardroom just outside San Francisco and took a seat at what appeared to be a lively table. I hadn't played in several months, and my hands seemed to welcome the feeling of holding the cards and handling the chips. It was exciting to peek at the cards I was dealt and devise a game plan. I felt a trace of guilt, but it was more than offset by that adrenaline rush I hadn't felt in so many months. The calling of the cards had pulled me in again. This would-be author, confessor of sins, and recovering addict was far from recovery.

* * *

For nearly two more years, I vigorously indulged my addiction. In those quiet conversations with my conscience, I told myself that this time I was in control. Poker was purely a pastime, an outlet for my competitive urges. I argued that because poker is largely a game of strategy—a psychological battle against the other players—it was good mental exercise that kept my mind sharp and my creative juices flowing, as long as I played with discipline and for modest stakes. That's not only what I told myself, it's also what I told my wife, my kids, and anyone who expressed concern.

Predictably enough, an old, familiar pattern recurred. My first few forays into the poker arena were profitable. And, because I had started on a winning note, it was easy for me to demonstrate discipline. I played only two- to three-hour sessions and maintained an otherwise normal daily routine of work, exercise, and sleep. What was equally important was that, at the time, I was content with playing at relatively small stakes. Of course, it was easy to maintain this kind of self-control when I was winning.

It didn't take long for my "new approach" to playing poker to change. I was at Commerce Casino for a weekend of fun and games at the world's most renowned poker room. There was a long waiting list for a seat at the medium-stakes games. So, feeling impatient, I ventured over to the higher-stakes area, where I was able to start playing right away. Instead of buying in for $400, which would have been standard in lower-stakes games, I bought in for $2,000 in the big boys' game. Even though that was the entire amount I had budgeted for the whole weekend, in this particular game, $2,000 made me the "shortest stack" at the table. Starting with my entire bankroll at risk was not a wise strategy, but exercising wisdom is not a defining trait of addicts.

As chance would have it, I dominated the table over the next few hours. When my $2,000 buy-in had grown to over $7,000, I gathered my chips, strode confidently to the cashier's window, and—with a bulging pocketful of cash—decided to take a break. I ran into a poker buddy of mine from San Francisco who had also just had a winning session of play, so we decided to splurge. He and his wife joined me for dinner and wine to celebrate our success at the tables.

When I returned to the poker room after about a four-hour break, my confidence was sky high. My pocketful of winnings was far more intoxicating than the two glasses of wine at dinner. At that very moment, I should have seen a red flag. Why go back to the big game? Why go back and play at all? I had nearly tripled my starting bankroll, enjoyed a relaxing dinner with friends, and ventured into hazardous territory, emerging (seemingly) unscathed. Why not get a good night's sleep and take an early flight home the next day? No, that was not to be. What followed that night, and for nearly another year, was a downward spiral that I believe was meant to be.

Chapter Ten

When I returned to the poker tables that night, I experienced a sequence of outcomes that defied mathematical probability. I entered hand after hand with the cards most likely to produce a winning result. A series of bets would then build a large pot, often containing a couple of thousand dollars or more. And then, with only one card remaining in the deck that could possibly give my opponent the winning hand, that "miracle card" would be dealt, and I would lose—repeatedly. This went on and on until my $7,000 stack had dwindled to about $1,500. Every losing hand caused greater anxiety. It was alarming. My pulse felt so strong that I was sure other players at the table could see the veins in my neck protruding—a sign of weakness and panic. At this point I could have left the high-stakes area and headed over to the lower-stakes games, where a mere $300 or $400 buy-in could have provided me all the action I wanted with a much lower and more manageable risk. But I chose the more daring, and dangerous, path.

I went to the ATM and took out about $2,500 in cash advances on my credit cards, and then returned to the scene of battle in the high-stakes game—hopeful, of course, that I could make a comeback. But this episode had a painful ending. I began to feel overwhelmed by a strange mix of emotions, from fear and guilt to anger and downright panic. Each layer threatened to plunge me into a darkness that I had been fighting off for years. I ended up pulling an all-nighter, and as night gave way to morning I made repeated trips to the ATM, but my luck didn't change. When I had finally exhausted my access to any additional cash with debit and credit cards, I gave up. Having lost over $5,000 on this trip, I returned home with an all-too-familiar feeling of dejection. I hadn't just fallen into this pit again, I had willingly jumped in, and I was overcome with fear that this time I might never be able to climb out.

Less than a year had passed since I had planted the seed of writing the Great American Autobiography, my story of renewal, redemption, and recovery, and Charlie had been right. In fact, relapse was not only possible, but, in my refusal to face the reality of my addiction, it became inevitable.

As the year 2013 rolled around, poker was consuming a huge part of my life. I was losing far more often than winning, sinking in a sea of debt, and spending a crazy amount of time at the tables. When work or weekend family plans prevented me from flying off to Las Vegas or down to Commerce, I spent Friday nights—sometimes Saturday mornings—playing at one of the local poker rooms. I am astonished that I managed to survive and maintain this pace, especially while repressing most of the emotional chaos brewing inside. I showed up at work every day with energy and enthusiasm, devoted time to community service, and had an active family life. At the same time, though, I spent many long days and nights chasing my poker losses and wondering how to put an end to this madness while maintaining my health, sanity, and dignity.

On one hand, the desperation I felt at this point was different from what I had experienced in the old high-roller days. I no longer had casino credit lines to juggle and manage, wasn't hundreds of thousands of dollars in debt, and had no tax delinquencies. On the other hand, I was in my mid-60s, financially insecure, and essentially living from paycheck to paycheck after more than four decades in a handsomely rewarding career. I had exhausted my savings and emptied a retirement account years earlier, while dealing with heavier debt. And now, because of my latest gambling relapse, I had zero net worth and plummeting self-respect. I felt stupid, irresponsible, and completely ashamed of myself. But there was an even more important consideration than money. How was my reckless, hard-core addiction affecting my most important relationships—with my children, my wife, and God?

I knew that Jason and Jessica loved and respected me, but I wanted so much for them to admire the kind of person their dad was. Yet, as long as I allowed gambling to drag me down, I wouldn't earn the admiration I longed for. As for Lyn—as it had been with my first wife, Diane—I knew that she loved and worried about me, but I thought she might be losing hope that I would ever get the monkey off my back. And what about my relationship with God? For me, everything begins and ends there. At the time, I prayed every day for guidance, mercy, forgiveness, and—if it was His will—a way out of my misery. But a true person of faith understands that God is not a genie who pops out of a bottle, grants our wishes, and then disappears until we think we need Him again. Living a life of faith means surrendering your life to God and not allowing selfish indulgences to be your master. I had to acknowledge in my talks with God that my heart still desired the occasional thrill of this thing that was destroying me, and I needed Him to take away that desire. I didn't expect this to happen overnight, but I had faith that it would happen.

My greatest concerns were truly those all-important relationships with God and my loved ones, but I still worried day and night about how to quickly stop the financial bleeding. My income was sufficient to cover ordinary bills and living expenses, but I also owed money to several personal friends who had lent me $3,000 here and $5,000 there to keep me afloat after a series of poker losses. The rational, ethical side of me was determined to honor my word and repay my friends in a timely fashion, but the side of me driven by addiction was still hoping for the big score that would make everything better.

Having always believed in honesty and in admitting my own poor choices, I turned to one of the friends who had lent me money. He also happens to be a poker player, so I hoped for a sympathetic ear. I laid bare my situation and explained that I was still in a hole financially and needed more time to pay him back. He was firm but understanding, and offered me a deal. He said it wasn't fair or wise for me to continue playing poker as long as I owed him money. So, he was willing to wait longer for me to pay him back if I would take a break from poker until he was fully repaid. I thought that was fair enough and felt greatly relieved. I had confronted the situation honestly, and it had a positive outcome.

I also had the sudden realization that I had not derived any thrill or pleasure from poker for a long time. Rather, I had been frantically playing a game of catch-up, a game I couldn't possibly win, chasing that elusive big score. Now, with extended time to repay my friend, I felt that my life was becoming a bit more manageable. I was confident I could stop playing poker for a while, which would permit me to get more rest and channel my energies into more productive pursuits. What a relief!

The success I had in being transparent with my friend prompted me to have similar heart-to-heart talks with Lyn and my kids, separately, of course. I wasn't sure what I expected to accomplish in those conversations, but I felt they had to happen. I was certain of two things, however—I wanted to show them the steps I was taking to distance myself from poker and get control of my life, and I wanted reassurance that I had their support and unconditional love. I must admit that I was a bit frightened. Jason and Jessica had heard me say so many times that I planned to rid my life of gambling. They had seen me take extended breaks, only to experience repeated relapses. Why should I expect them to have greater faith in my resolve this time, after I had repeatedly dashed their hopes? I desperately ached for my children to believe in me, but I feared that they no longer could. That fear was painful and scary. And as for Lyn, I was confident that she would be encouraging, but I doubted whether she could still believe in me either.

My prayers and candid conversations were important steps in getting control of my life, but now I had to follow through—I had to deliver the goods, and the first person I had to convince was myself.

Chapter Eleven

On Sunday, January 4, 2015, I gambled for the last time—
ever! I placed the final bet of my life.

I had just spent Christmas with my kids in New York and, New Year's back in San Francisco with Lyn. My daughter, Jessica, was pregnant and due to deliver my first grandchild in June. And I was experiencing a wide range of emotions. The holiday season had been filled with joy and fond family memories, but I felt anxious and depressed about how broke I was after holiday spending. While talking with Jessica about the prospect of grandfatherhood, I promised that gambling would be completely out of my life before my grandchild was born, that her baby's grandfather would not be a gambler. Jessica breathed a quiet sigh and said, "I hope not. I know you mean that, Dad. I just . . . hope not." Those few words spoke volumes.

I had several hours to wrestle with my conscience during the return flight to California. I was sincere in my promise to Jessica. I could not let her child be born into a world where Grandpa was a gambler. That was a promise I would keep. I can't describe why I felt so certain about this after so many broken promises in the past. There was just a steeliness in my resolve that I had not felt before.

But my demons weren't done with me. The dark side of my heart presented me a loophole. Why not take just one more crack at poker right now, and then walk away? That wouldn't be breaking my promise, I rationalized, because Jessica's due date was more than six months away. Furthermore, a nice win might cover my holiday expenditures. This is the twisted logic that resides in the mind of an addict.

On Saturday, January 3, I headed down to Commerce Casino in LA. I had a bad feeling in the pit of my stomach about this trip from the very moment I decided to go. Once I arrived, though, I tried to suppress that desperate feeling of *needing* to win, and allowed myself to be fueled by the foolish optimism that often overtakes gamblers at the beginning of a session. "This is a new day," I told myself. "I have to put previous losses out of my mind. If I can manage to win big early on, I won't even stay overnight—I'll just cash in, go home, and end my poker-playing career on a winning note." I kept feeding myself these thoughts, even as my rational side kept waving red flags.

I decided to play in the big game, in the high-stakes area. All the tables were filled, so I put my name on the waiting list for a seat. Apparently, other holiday revelers were there to recoup a few bucks, just as I was. This was comforting, as I knew I wasn't the only "desperado" in the room. Finally, with a long waiting list of eager players, the poker room managers opened up another table and I was able to take a seat. I bought in for $4,000—money I could ill afford to lose—and was ready for action. It was late afternoon. As evening approached, the waning daylight bled into the casino through the front entrance doors, giving the room a sort of amber glow. It gave me a warm, relaxed feeling. Deal the cards!

It took less than an hour for my confidence to be shaken. I hadn't lost a large amount of money on any single hand, but my stack of chips had diminished in a drip, drip, drip of small losses. So, I took a brief break from the action and walked over to the concession area to get a cappuccino, hoping that would help me get refocused. Five minutes later, my spirits renewed, I was back in my seat.

The very first hand I played after returning to the table generated lots of betting and raising. With nine players at the table, and the pot growing so large on the first round of betting, players holding mediocre hands will generally fold (toss away their cards) quickly. In this case, four players, including me, remained in the hand until the final card was dealt. At this point, a familiar player known as a notorious bluffer announced, "All-in!" He then shoved his entire stack of chips forward, totaling about $8,000. It was an intimidating bet, because each of the remaining three of us had less than half of that amount, so calling his bet would have put our entire bankrolls at risk. The two other players quickly folded. I felt confident that I held the winning hand and that Mr. Bluffer was living up to his reputation. I called his bet and nervously pushed forward my remaining stack, about $2,500. He wasn't bluffing. I lost the hand and all of my chips.

I felt like I had been punched in the stomach. I let out an audible sigh, and all of the breath seemed to leave my body. I was unable to speak. I inhaled in a kind of gasping fashion and tried to compose myself. My heart was racing. Suddenly, I felt very foolish. Why had I thought this guy was bluffing? Shouldn't I have developed a better "read" on him as that hand had progressed? What now? Leave the table in defeat, or reload and give it another shot? I stood up, as players often do after losing their entire stack, and said to the dealer, "Hold my seat," which means, "I'll be right back." I walked around the building, trying to calm myself as I engaged in the old, familiar internal debate about what to do.

I gave little consideration to the most sensible option—going home. Another option was to go to my hotel room, get a good night's sleep, and return to the poker room fresh the next morning. I chose the third option—access more cash at the ATM and get back in the game. Scraping together another $3,500, I re-entered the arena of combat and invested all of my energy and concentration in mounting a comeback.

By 8:00 that evening, I was back in action. I played a bit more cautiously with my second buy-in, looking for good betting opportunities and taking only minimal risks. This more conservative approach, known as "playing tight," helped me avoid significant swings up or down as I played until nearly 5:00 a.m. Having survived an all-night session with my bank-roll relatively undiminished, I retired to my room for a couple of hours of sleep.

I woke up just after 8:00 a.m. Having slept just under three hours, I was wide-eyed, restless, and eager to play for a while before my afternoon flight home. I showered, got dressed, packed my overnight bag, and went down to the front desk to check out early. Just in case I ended up playing until it was time to leave for the airport, I wouldn't have to waste time going back to my room or standing in a checkout line. All I had to do for the next few hours was play poker. If this was going to be my last session ever, I wanted to maximize my playing time. That was my plan, but the sequence of events that unfolded sent me packing in a matter of minutes.

The very first hand I played generated lots of betting. As a huge pile of chips grew in the center of the table, I was left facing only one opponent. Half of my stack was invested in this pot. I desperately needed to win this one. But the last card to leave the dealer's hand delivered defeat to me and that big pile of chips to my opponent. Now, with my bankroll cut in half, I was hoping for an opportunity to go all-in with a winning hand. That was my only realistic chance to bounce back.

I didn't have to wait long. Within five minutes, I found myself with a very strong hand. I was holding three of a kind against a player who was drawing to a flush, five cards in the same suit, which would beat my hand. The other player announced, "All-in." I quickly called his bet, as the odds favored me at this point. There was just one more card to be dealt. What followed was surreal. That last card seemed to float from the dealer's fingers in slow motion, like a scene from a movie, and then it landed on the table with a thud. It was, of course, just the card my opponent needed. He made his flush, my chips were all gone, and I was in a momentary state of numbness.

I felt lost and confused as I stood up to leave the table. My first few steps were weak and tentative, but then a strange thing happened. My stride became stronger and steadier as I got closer to exiting the poker room. Somehow, walking out of that casino was like escaping a torture chamber. Of course, I felt defeated and dejected about the money I had lost and about having made the trip to Commerce in the first place, but I also felt strangely relieved. Somehow, I had this comforting knowledge that my long, debilitating journey had ended. I wasn't sure at that moment how I knew I had placed my last bet, but I felt possessed by a sense of finality I had not known before. I was done with gambling.

Now, in the winter of my life and career, I had to change course in a profound and lasting way. Where to begin?

Chapter Twelve

I had already checked out of my room, but it was several hours before my flight home was scheduled to depart and I needed to find a quiet, private place where I could collect my thoughts and figure out how to begin, once and for all, living a life free of gambling. I asked the front-desk attendant if I could return to my room for a while, since it was still long before checkout time. She said okay and gave me a key. When I got to the room, I fell to my knees and began to pray. First, I gave thanks for arriving at this point of brokenness. It was clear that I had to hit rock bottom before I would truly want to quit gambling. I then asked God to instill in me a desire to quit—to let my pain, shame, and guilt strengthen my resolve. I prayed for comfort, strength, and forgiveness. And I asked for guidance in repairing any damage I had done to my most treasured relationships—with my children, my wife, and friends who had watched me struggle with my addiction for so many years.

The very next thing I did after praying was call Lyn. I didn't know whether she would react with anger or sympathy, but I knew that I had to tell her everything—how much money I had lost, that I had maxed out my credit cards, and that I needed her love and support in my recovery. Lyn's response was just the medicine I needed. She sensed something in the tone of my voice and the words I spoke that told her I really meant it this time. She was going to hold me accountable, but she reassured me of her unconditional love and support. I had now completed step two in shedding the oppressive weight of my guilt.

The next step was to call an old poker buddy, Ray, who had once given me a bridge loan to get me through some financial strain. I hid nothing from Ray, as I confessed the stupidity of my decision to give poker "one more shot" after the Christmas visit with my family, and told him all the sad details of my Commerce experience. Having convinced myself, at least, that I would never gamble again, I asked Ray to help me out one last time until the cash flow from my income allowed me to get back on track financially. He gave me a stern, heartfelt lecture, said he actually believed I was committed this time, and agreed to lend me the cash I needed.

The half hour or so I spent in that hotel room baring my soul was more than cathartic—it was restorative. I headed to the airport and boarded my flight home without the crushing sadness and uncertainty I had felt after so many losing trips over the years. However, when I got home that evening, I had to swim through a flood of emotions. I felt angry at myself for having lived on the edge for over three decades, putting everything precious to me at risk—my family, career, health, reputation, financial stability, and spiritual growth. I also felt sad. In a few months, I was going to be 68 years old. Yet, in a sense, I was starting all over again. What kind of fool allows this to happen? And there was the fear factor. Life is fragile and uncertain. I was afraid that I might not have enough time left to live up to my promises, salvage my reputation, or provide some measure of financial stability for my family. But I was certain of one thing—I knew where to begin.

I needed to return to the core values I learned in childhood. Those values had never failed me. Compulsive gambling had brought out the worst characteristics in my nature: willfulness, wastefulness, greed, excessive pride, indiscretion, and a whole host of qualities that were antithetical to all that I professed to believe in—the sound values that had sustained me in all circumstances.

During this period of soul-searching, I had no thoughts of playing poker or of gambling in any form. That was reaffirming, as I knew that only my behavior, and not my repeated promises, would be meaningful to my family. My thoughts during this time often took me back to my childhood. I remembered the amazing role models my parents were in the face of adversity. I recalled their strength and resilience, hard work and sacrifice, discipline and devotion, and their emphasis on honesty and accountability. They had admonished me throughout my childhood to always tell the truth when I "messed up," and to accept responsibility for my actions. My mom and dad had no patience for the victimhood mentality. Even though black people in the Old South were certainly victims of a vicious and hateful system of racism and discrimination, my parents taught my brother and me never to think of ourselves as victims. We were strivers, striving to overcome unfair and unfortunate circumstances. And certainly, when dealing with circumstances within our control, we were not even to consider playing the victim card.

So, reflecting on this childhood lesson was a huge step in my willingness to confront my gambling addiction. No one had twisted my arm or seduced me into this pattern of behavior.

I had freely chosen this self-destructive path, and I needed to man up and own it. At the same time, though, I couldn't let myself be consumed by guilt or self-pity, and I didn't. I devoted those first few months after my last bet to healthier pursuits. I resumed working out regularly, which made me feel stronger and more clear-headed. I found renewed energy for weekend getaways with Lyn. And my prayer time became more mean- ingful, as I began relying more on God's guidance.

During those years of playing poker, succumbing to the futility of chasing lost fortunes, my prayer time was missing a fundamental aspect of connecting with God. That missing aspect was surrender—turning all things over to Him, knowing that He would provide strength and direction. While pray- ing, I would often acknowledge that I wished the misery from gambling to go away, but deep down in my heart I still had the desire to gamble. So, as my poker losses had dragged me deeper and deeper into a pit of despair, I had begun asking God to change my heart, to take away my desire to gamble. I prayed for the resolve to give it up and walk away while I was still healthy. And I prayed for the strength and wisdom to be a better role model for my children and grandchildren-to-be.

As Jessica's due date in June of 2015 approached, I felt less like an addict and more like a recovering addict. I not only felt no desire to play poker again, but was eager to model my values and beliefs—my better self—for the sake of the new addition to our family. On June 8, little Noah was born, and I fell profoundly and indescribably in love, just as I had when Jason and Jessica were born. My time and attention, apart from work, were now intensely focused on my growing family.

* * *

By the time Noah was a year old, my renewed devotion to family, work, and spiritual growth had enabled me to erase much of my poker-inflicted debt, while not missing the empty thrill or "rush" I had sought during my gambling days.

But before going any further in describing my road to recovery, I want to be very clear about something. I do not claim to be cured of my addiction. Psychologists tend to agree that addicts are never cured, but that they can avoid relapse, remain clean, and live as recovering addicts. Furthermore, I acknowledge that I have not sought psychological counseling for gambling in recent years, nor have I entered any prescribed or recognized programs designed to treat addiction. In no way am I suggesting that the path I followed in dealing with gambling is a viable alternative to seeking professional help from certified counselors. I am not sharing my story as a prescription for treating addiction of any kind.

Here's why I *am* sharing my story. I want my life to serve as a source of comfort and inspiration for people facing challenges and difficulty of any kind. No matter where we come from or what station we achieve in life, no one enjoys perfect peace. No one is without worry, fear, pain, anxiety, or self-doubt. Everyone experiences sadness, heartbreak, failure, embarrassment, and uncertainty. In many ways, the human condition is frail and flawed. Yet, in many other ways, the human spirit is strong, resilient, hopeful, and resourceful. On the surface, my life may read like a storybook version of the American Dream. A poor, black kid from the Jim Crow South overcomes untold hardship and adversity and rises to prominence as a high-salaried national television personality. He makes his parents proud, provides a comfortable life for his family, and is recognized every day by adoring fans. He probably has no idea what it's like to feel powerless, worthless, invisible, or insecure, right? Well, if you've arrived at this point in the book, you know that's not true.

I reached many low points during my three decades of gambling—two Chapter 7 bankruptcies, loss of a home to the IRS, shattered self-esteem, damaged personal relationships, and spiritual decay. I offer my life story not as a prescription, but as an example of how it's never too late to begin turning your life around. What worked for me will not work for everyone, but I hope my story demonstrates that even in the face of hardship, grief, depression, or addiction, recovery is achievable, self-esteem can be restored, and relationships can be rebuilt. My road map to recovery was charted by recommitting to those things that had always been unfailing sources of comfort, strength, and joy—family, faith, and fundamental values. But consider how far I had to fall before I came to my senses and made smart choices. Gambling held such a strong grip on me that I had to become a broken man—staring mortality in the face, living paycheck to paycheck, worrying about how I'd be remembered by my children.

Given my stumbles and backsliding, it is reasonable to question how I can possibly know that I won't gamble again. After all, I did begin writing this book in 2012, only to have that writing interrupted by another relapse. I can only tell you that I am committed to living a purposeful life, and the closer I get to the end of this life, the deeper my commitment is. My conscience will no longer permit me to break the promises I've made. I've promised Jason and Jessica, Diane and Lyn, and even little Noah—although he doesn't understand it yet—that I will never gamble again. Living up to that promise is far more important to me than any momentary thrill I might get from raking in a stack of chips after a winning bet. But perhaps most meaningful of all is the commitment I made to God to live the remainder of my life with a greater sense of purpose—a purpose found in those values my parents taught me in childhood, a purpose found in that which is eternal, not that which is temporary. Will I keep my promise never to gamble again? You bet your life!